Older Migrants – Vulnerable and Excluded

Ius, Lex et Res Publica
Studies in Law, Philosophy and Political Cultures

Edited by Barbara Janusz-Pohl and Anna Jaron

Volume 35

Barbara Mikołajczyk

Older Migrants – Vulnerable and Excluded

Searching for Visibility in Universal and European Laws

PETER LANG

Berlin - Bruxelles - Chennai - Lausanne - New York - Oxford

Bibliographic Information published by the Deutsche Nationalbibliothek
The Deutsche Nationalbibliothek lists this publication in the Deutsche Nationalbibliografie; detailed bibliographic data is available in the internet at http://dnb.d-nb.de.

Library of Congress Cataloging-in-Publication Data
A CIP catalog record for this book has been applied for at the Library of Congress.

The publication was produced as a part of project no.2018/ 31/ B/ HS5/ 00435 (OPUS 16) – financed by the National Science Centre, Poland and conducted at the University of Silesia in Katowice.

Cover illustration: Courtesy of Benjamin Ben Chaim.

UNIVERSITY OF SILESIA
IN KATOWICE

ISSN 2191-3250
ISBN 978-3-631-92460-0 (Print)
E-ISBN 978-3-631-92461-7 (E-Book)
E-ISBN 978-3-631-92648-2 (E-PUB)
DOI 10.3726/b22335

Published by Peter Lang GmbH, Berlin, Deutschland

info@peterlang.com - www.peterlang.com

This publication has been peer reviewed.
www.peterlang.com

Table of Contents

Abbreviations 7

Introduction 11

1. "An older migrant" in the international agenda 19

2. Older migrants and the various faces of vulnerability 25
   - 2.1. Attempts at conceptualisation 25
   - 2.2. An inexhaustible list of vulnerabilities 29

3. The starting point: Non-discrimination and the triad of obligations 41
   - 3.1. Universal pillars 41
   - 3.2. European developments 55
   - 3.3. Potential for filling gaps 65

4. Lex specialis 77
   - 4.1. Older voluntary migrants 77
   - 4.2. Older persons in forced migration 89

5. Proposed interpretative tools 101
   - 5.1. *Pacta sunt servanda* and good faith principles 101
   - 5.2. The conceptual output of international bodies 103

Final remarks 113

Annexe 117
A. Global forum 117
B. Regional forums 125
I. Council of Europe 125
II. European Union 128
III. Organization of American States 135
IV. African Union 136

References 137
Bibliography 137
Treaties 149
Jurisprudence 153
Resolutions, recommendations and other soft documents 154
Human Rights Council procedures 159
EU Law 160
Other documents 164
Reports 166

Abbreviations

CEAS	Common European Asylum System
CED	Committee on Enforced Disappearances
CEDAW	Convention on the Elimination of All Forms of Discrimination against Women
CEDAW Committee	Committee on the Elimination of Discrimination against Women
CESCR	Committee on Economic, Social and Cultural Rights
CETS	Council of Europe Treaty Series
CFREU	Charter of Fundamental Rights in the European Union
CJEU	Court of Justice of the European Union
CMW	Committee on the Protection of the Rights of All Migrant Workers and Members of their Families
CoE	Council of Europe
CRC	Committee on the Rights of the Child
CRPD	Convention on the Rights of Persons with Disabilities
CRPD Committee	Committee on the Rights of Persons with Disabilities
ECHR	Convention for the Protection of Human Rights and Fundamental Freedoms/ European Convention on Human Rights
ECSR	European Committee of Social Rights
ECtHR	European Court of Human Rights
ESC	European Social Charter of 1961
ESC (Revised)	European Social Charter of 1996
EU	European Union
EUAA	European Union Agency for Asylum
FRA	Fundamental Rights Agency
HRBA	human rights-based approach
HRC	Human Rights Committee

ICCPR	International Covenant on Civil and Political Rights
ICESCR	International Covenant on Economic, Social and Cultural Rights
IDC	International Detention Coalition
IIL	Institute of International Law
ILO	International Labour Organisation
IOM	International Organization for Migration
EEA	European Economic Area
EFTA	European Free Trade Association
ECRI	European Commission against Racism and Intolerance
UN Independent Expert/IEOP	UN Independent Expert on the enjoyment of all human rights by older persons
LNOB	"leave no one behind"
MIPAA	Madrid International Plan of Action on Ageing
NGOs	non-governmental organisations
OJ	Official Journal
OAS	Organization of American States
OECD	Organisation for Economic Cooperation and Development
OEWGA	UN Open-ended Working Group on Ageing
PACE	Council of Europe Parliamentary Assembly
para.	paragraph
Rec.	recommendation
RES	resolution
RESC	Revised European Social Charter
ROSEnet	Reducing Old-Age Social Exclusion: Collaborations in Research and Policy
SDG	Sustainable Development Goal
TEU	Treaty on European Union
TFEU	Treaty on the Functioning of the European Union
UDHR	Universal Declaration of Human Rights
UHRI	Universal Human Rights Index
UN	United Nations

UNDESA	United Nations Department of Economic and Social Affairs
UNDG	United Nations Development Group
UNDP	United Nations Development Programme
UNECE	United Nations Economic Commission for Europe
UNESCO	United Nations Educational, Scientific and Cultural Organisation
UNFPA	United Nations Population Fund
UNGA/UN General Assembly	United Nations General Assembly
UN-Habitat	United Nations Human Settlements Programme
UNHCHR	United Nations High Commissioner for Human Rights
UNHCR	United Nations High Commissioner for Refugees
UNTS	United Nations Treaty Series
UPR	Universal Periodic Review
VCLT	Vienna Convention on the Law of Treaties
WHO	World Health Organization

Introduction

According to the United Nations Department of Economic and Social Affairs (UNDESA) by 2050, one in six people in the world will be over the age of 65, up from one in ten in 2021.[1] This demographic change is irreversible and has inevitable consequences for economies, industry, health and social care, and security systems. Various aspects of global ageing and its impact on societies and economies have been analysed in many international reports and scholarship.[2] In the contemporary world, these demographic changes and intensive population movements overlap. The juxtaposition of these phenomena has a variety of consequences, including a growing number of older people who are "on the move."

Migrant populations, as whole societies, are ageing. The Global Migration Analysis Centre reported that 12.2 % of international migrants (34.3 million people) are aged 65 and over.[3] The recent OECD report shows that, in the EU and the OECD, this category of migrants consists of about 15 % of the foreign-born population.[4]

---

1 *World Population Prospects 2022: Summary of Results* (New York: United Nations, 2022).

2 For example: "World Social Report: Leaving No One behind in an Ageing World", No E.23.IV.2 (New York, NY: United Nations, 2023); Suzanne Kunkel et al., eds., *Global Aging: Comparative Perspectives on Aging and the Life Course* (New York: Springer Publishing Company, 2014); OECD/European Commission, "Integration of the Elderly Immigrant Population, in: Indicators of Immigrant Integration" (Paris, 2023), https://www.oecd-ilibrary.org/docserver/044e2698-en.pdf?expires=1703869677&id=id&accname=guest&checksum=8B8068507F193D88770A79E3D70C79D6., Jason L. Powell, *Globalization and Global Aging* (New York: Novinka, 2013), Frans J. Willekens, "Demographic Transitions in Europe and the World", 0 ed. (Rostock: Max Planck Institute for Demographic Research, March 2014), https://doi.org/10.4054/MPIDR-WP-2014-004.

3 International Organization for Migration's Global Migration Data Analysis Centre, "Migration Data Portal", 2022, https://www.migrationdataportal.org/themes/older-persons-and-migration.

4 OECD et al., "Immigrant Civic Engagement and Social Integration", 2023, 151.

In high- and middle-income countries, their number escalated by nearly 16 million from mid-1990 to mid-2020, while in low-income countries, it only increased by 76,587. Between 1990 and 2020, the number of older migrants rose by 3,4 % in Europe[5] and 2,1 % in North America.[6] The newcomers are also older than those arriving in the past. The Center for Immigration Studies of Census Bureau data showed that the age at which immigrants are arriving in the USA has increased dramatically since 2000. The share of newcomers 55 and older in 2019 was 11 %, double the 5 % in 2000. Meanwhile, in the case of migrants 65 + the percentage was 6 % in 2019, compared to just 2 % in 2000.[7]

Meanwhile, both migrants and older people are heterogeneous groups. They are people of various experiences, ages, genders, ethnicities and diverse legal statuses, health conditions, skills, etc. This multiplied heterogeneity of older migrants causes them to be invisible when gathering various data types and their specific needs are not recognised. What is most important from the perspective of this study is that this situation leaves them vulnerable to human rights violations. Thus, migration in older age, as well as ageing outside the home country, is also an issue of international human rights law. However, older migrants often escape international human rights regulations and determining the obligations of states to respect, protect and fulfil the human rights of older people "on the move" is very difficult.

Therefore, the combination of age and other grounds for discrimination, including migration status, needs more research from various perspectives.[8] Several studies have been published in recent years on specific aspects of the migratory situation of older people, in particular the ageing and social exclusion of older migrants in host countries. For example, on issues such as the burden of migrants and war refugees on national budgets, social

5 Worth noting is also the increase of 3,7 % in the Oceania region.

6 International Organization for Migration's Global Migration Data Analysis Centre, "Migration Data Portal", https://www.migrationdataportal.org/themes/older-persons-and-migration.

7 Steven A. Camarota and Karen Zeigler, "Immigrants Coming to America at Older Ages. A Look at Age at Arrival among New Immigrants, 2000 to 2019" (Washington, D.C.: Center for Immigration Studies, 2021).

8 Alan Gutterman, "Intersectionality and Rights of Older Persons", *SSRN Electronic Journal*, 2023, 8, https://doi.org/10.2139/ssrn.4024373.

pensions for migrants, social, medical and long-term care, ageism towards older migrants,[9] as well as reunification with older family members remaining in a country of origin.[10] It is worth noting the research on "the triply (at least) vulnerable" groups, including older migrant women[11] and older non-heteronormative migrants.[12]

However, these examples refer only to particular aspects of the intersection of migration and ageing, whereas the theoretical and practical threads at this intersection are comprehensively explored in the "Handbook on Migration and Ageing", edited by Sandra Torres and Alistair Hunter (2023).[13] It is a profound interdisciplinary study that analyses on the intersectionality of ageing and migration, including issues related to intergenerational relations, ethnicity, diversity and the intersectionality of ageing and migration, integration, social exclusion, ageing in host countries, racism, stereotyping, international retirement, loneliness, access to services

---

9 Pnina Dolberg, Sigurveig H. Sigurđardóttir, and Ursula Trummer, "Ageism and Older Immigrants", in *Contemporary Perspectives on Ageism Edited by Liat Aylon and Clemens Tesh – Romer* (Springer, Cham, 2018), 177–91.

10 Heli Askola, "(No) Migrating for Family Care in Later Life: Senchishak v Finland, Older Parents and Family Reunification", *European Journal of Migration and Law* 18, No. 3 (20 September 2016): 351–72, https://doi.org/10.1163/15718166-12342106.

11 Hafifa Siddiq, Qais Alemi, and Eunice Lee, "A Qualitative Inquiry of Older Afghan Refugee Women's Individual and Sociocultural Factors of Health and Health Care Experiences in the United States", *Journal of Transcultural Nursing* 34, No. 2 (March 2023): 143–50, https://doi.org/10.1177/10436596221149692; Natasha Reid et al., "Frailty in Ethnic Minority Women", *Maturitas* 152 (October 2021): 26–31, https://doi.org/10.1016/j.maturitas.2021.07.005. Ayat Nashwan, Sherry M Cummings, and Kara Gagnon, "Older Female Iraqi Refugees in the United States: Voices of Struggle and Strength", *International Social Work* 62, No. 2 (March 2019): 653–68, https://doi.org/10.1177/0020872817742699.

12 Yiu Tung Suen, "Ageing Non-Heterosexual Migrants: Towards Global Sexual Citizenship", *Journal of Aging Studies* 60 (March 2022): 100980, https://doi.org/10.1016/j.jaging.2021.100980.

13 Sandra Torres and Alistair Hunter, eds., *Handbook on Migration and Ageing*, Elgar Handbooks in Migration (Cheltenham, UK ; Northampton, MA, USA: Edward Elgar Publishing, 2023).

and many others. The works of Russell King and colleagues[14] also deserve particular attention, most notably "Unpacking the ageing-migration nexus and challenging the vulnerability trope" (2017),[15] in which they bring to light the nexus between ageing and migration and look at "older people left behind by migration."[16]

However, the area of human rights law and older migrants from the perspective of international law appears to still be relatively unexplored. One of the few texts on the subject is the chapter "Sidestepping Rights: An Analysis of the Intersection of Human Rights Obligations and Their Practical Implications for Older Migrants" by Ada Lui Gallassi and Lars Harrysson in the book by Kieran Walsh and colleagues "Social Exclusion in Later Life" (2021).[17]

That is why this study aims to establish whether and how international human rights law protects older migrants and what the states' obligations are in this regard. Traditionally, the international community agrees that states have the right to decide on their own migration policies. However, international human rights law establishes some limits on the states' freedom in this area. In 2017, the Human Rights Council stressed that states "have a duty to comply with their obligations under relevant international law, including international human rights law and refugee law, in order to ensure full respect for the human rights of migrants, including migrants in a vulnerable situation."[18]

---

14 Russell King and Aija Lulle, "Ageing, Migration, and Development", in *Routledge Handbook of Migration and Development*, ed. Tanja Bastia and Ronald Skeldon, Routledge International Handbooks (London New York: Routledge, Taylor & Francis Group, 2020), 211–20.

15 Russell King et al., "Unpacking the Ageing–Migration Nexus and Challenging the Vulnerability Trope", *Journal of Ethnic and Migration Studies* 43, No. 2 (25 January 2017): 182–98, https://doi.org/10.1080/1369183X.2016.1238904.

16 King et al., 185.

17 Ada Lui Gallassi and Lars Harrysson, "Sidestepping Rights: An Analysis of the Intersection of Human Rights Obligations and Their Practical Implications for Older Migrants", in *Social Exclusion in Later Life*, ed. Kieran Walsh et al., vol. 28, International Perspectives on Aging (Cham: Springer International Publishing, 2021), 275–86, https://doi.org/10.1007/978-3-030-51406-8_21.

18 Human Rights Council, "Resolution Adopted by the Human Rights Council on 22 June 2017 35/17. Protection of the Human Rights of Migrants: The Global Compact for Safe, Orderly and Regular Migration, 6 July 2017, A/HRC/RES/

Thus, the relationship between migration management and the protection of human rights is not straightforward, as evidenced by the reluctance of states to adopt the Convention on the Protection of the Rights of All Migrant Workers and Members of Their Families of 1990,[19] which was (and in many cases still is) linked to questioning their obligation to respect the human rights of undocumented migrants.[20]

International human rights law, along with the Universal Declaration of Human Rights (UDHR),[21] the International Covenant on Economic, Social and Cultural Rights (ICESCR)[22] and the International Covenant on Civil and Political Rights (ICCPR)[23] as well as principal regional human rights treaties[24] in the forefront, are certainly in place to protect the human rights of every person in every life situation. After all, the UDHR states that all

35/17", https://www.un.org/en/development/desa/population/migration/generalassembly/docs/globalcompact/A_HRC_RES_35_17.pdf.

19 United Nations, "International Convention on the Protection of the Rights of All Migrant Workers and Members of Their Families New York, 18 December 1990, Doc. A/RES/45/158." (UNTS, vol. 2220, p. 3), https://treaties.un.org/Pages/ViewDetails.aspx?src=TREATY&mtdsg_no=IV-13&chapter=4&clang=_en.

20 Graziano Battistella, in *Migration and Human Rights: The United Nations Convention on Migrant Workers' Rights*, ed. Ryszard Cholewinski, Antoine Pécoud, and Paul de Guchteneire, 1. publ, UNESCO Publishing (Cambridge: Cambridge University Press [u.a.], 2009), 66.

21 UN General Assembly, "Universal Declaration of Human Rights Adopted by the United Nations General Assembly in Paris on 10 December 1948 General Assembly Resolution 217 A.", https://www.un.org/en/ga/search/view_doc.asp?symbol=A/RES/217(III).

22 United Nations, "International Covenant on Economic, Social and Cultural Rights New York, 16 December 1966", UNTS vol. 993, p. 3, https://treaties.un.org/Pages/ViewDetails.aspx?src=IND&mtdsg_no=IV-3&chapter=4.

23 United Nations, "International Covenant on Civil and Political Rights, New York, 16 December 1966" (UNTS vol. 999, p. 171 and vol. 1057, p. 407).

24 Council of Europe, "Convention for the Protection of Human Rights and Fundamental Freedoms, Rome, 4 November 1950" (European Treaty Series No. 005, 1950); Organization of African Unity, "African Charter on Human and Peoples' Rights (Banjul Charter) Adopted 27 June 1981, Organisation of African Unity, Doc. CAB/LEG/67/3 Rev. 5, 21" (21 International Legal Materials 58, 1981), https://www.achpr.org/legalinstruments/detail?id=49. Organization of American States, "American Convention on Human Rights, 'Pact of San Jose,' Costa Rica, 22 November 1969, (B-32)", 1969.

people everywhere in the world are "born free and equal in dignity and rights," (Article 1) and are therefore rights-holders.

The central premise of this study is that, if international and European laws are to influence states to include older migrants' needs in ageing and migration policies, then older migrants should be identified at an international level. However, older migrants are currently invisible in treaty law and, if the law is to attempt to protect them, it needs guidance from international bodies and relevant interpretation of existing legal provisions. That is why, this study aims to identify international norms protecting (at least potentially) older migrants and indicate interpretative tools to improve the ability of international human rights law, and consequently national laws, to respond to the vulnerabilities of older migrants.

The main areas of research are universal and regional, mainly European hard and soft laws, as well as the output of the international human rights bodies. Universal law and European laws, covering the regional international law and European Union law, are major areas of interest, as we are currently witnessing the emergence of international law on older persons on a global forum, and the new approach to migration expressed in documents adopted as a result of the migration crisis of 2015–2016.[25] EU law is taken into account here because it is EU solutions that affect the migration situation throughout Europe and other regions of the world. In addition, the human right to asylum is firmly anchored in EU law. At the same time, it is not uncommon for the application of EU asylum law to create tensions with the European Convention for the Protection of Human Rights and Fundamental Freedoms (European Convention for Human Rights, ECHR).[26] Moreover, the European migration and asylum law is also changing, as the EU Member States have been in a permanent migration crisis for a decade, given that some of them are the largest destinations

25 Anna Doliwa-Klepacka, "The New Pact on Migration and Asylum as a Response to Current Migration Challenges – Selected Issues", *Białostockie Studia Prawnicze* 26, no. 1 (1 March 2021): 9–21, https://doi.org/10.15290/bsp.2021.26.01.01.

26 Evangelia (Lilian) Tsourdi and Cathryn Costello, "'Systemic Violations' in EU Asylum Law: Cover or Catalyst?", *German Law Journal* 24, no. 6 (September 2023): 982–94, https://doi.org/10.1017/glj.2023.59.

for international migrants.[27] Thus, it is a challenge for societies, states and European organisations to cope with migration pressure, including those artificially created by the Russian Federation and Belarus,[28] flows of refugees and war refugees from Ukraine and other parts of the world, along with economic and climate migration from everywhere. Therefore, in December 2023, the European Union Member States, after years of negotiations, agreed on the New Pact on Migration and Asylum, a set of binding instruments and policies to create a fairer, more efficient and more sustainable migration and asylum process for the European Union. Among other things, it is supposed to establish a common approach to migration and asylum that is based on solidarity, responsibility and respect for human rights.[29] However, it is becoming challenging for Europe, which is the fastest ageing continent, to cope with aged migrants and newcomers.

Before one can trace the protection of older migrants under global and European laws, it is important to establish who is considered an older migrant and what types of migrants are recognised in international forums and law. As international human rights law aims to protect the most vulnerable, this study focuses mainly on those older migrants at the greatest risk of having their human rights violated. Then the research is divided into parts dedicated to establishing the standard of protection of voluntary and involuntary migrants. The last chapter sets out proposals for the interpretation of international law norms to make older migrants visible to various stakeholders, in particular states when creating their social and immigration policies. Finally, given that the identification of international and European law (soft and hard) relating to older people in a migratory situation may present some difficulties, this study is supplemented by a selection of international documents and provisions dedicated directly to older voluntary

27 *World Migration Report 2022* (International Organization for Migration (IOM), 2021), 24.

28 Aleksandra Jolkina, "Migrant Instrumentalisation: Facts and Fictions", *Verfassungsblog: On Matters Constitutional*, 21 September 2023, https://doi.org/10.17176/20230921-223514-0.

29 European Commission, "Communication from the Commission on a New Pact on Migration and Asylum Brussels, 23.9.2020 COM(2020) 609 Final" (European Union, 2020), https://eur-lex.europa.eu/legal-content/EN/TXT/HTML/?uri=CELEX:52020DC0609.

and involuntary migrants that may facilitate the establishment of a standard for their protection. However, the study will also include references to the output of other international organisations, particularly the work of the Organization of American States, as it was in this forum that the most advanced treaty protecting older persons was adopted.

This research is part of a bigger project[30] dedicated to the inclusion of older people under international human rights law and pays special attention to the intersectionality of exclusion.[31] For this reason, the study may be useful for public authorities at various levels, as well as for civil society organisations and academia in general.

30 Project no. 2018/31/B/HS5/00435 (OPUS 16) – "Social and digital inclusion of older people as a special task for NGOs. A perspective of international human rights law" – financed by the National Science Centre, Poland.

31 Barbara Mikołajczyk, *Social Inclusion for Older Persons and Human Rights Law. The Potential for Universal and European Instruments* (Wydawnictwo Uniwersytetu Śląskiego, 2023), https://wydawnictwo.us.edu.pl/sites/wydawnictwo.us.edu.pl/files/wus_2023_mikolajczyk_social_inclusion_for_older_persons_ebook.pdf.

1. "An older migrant" in the international agenda

Defining an "older migrant" is not an easy task for an international lawyer. The law, including international law, usually tends to define all objects and subjects, including "older persons" and "old age." Meanwhile, "age" is not a unifying factor in describing somebody as an older person, because older persons are of diverse ages. Differences in life expectancy are still enormous (up to 30 years) among states and continents, and sometimes within particular countries and regions.[32] Being old in Africa means something quite different from, for example, being old in Europe or Japan.[33] Moreover, the vulnerability of this vast and heterogeneous category of persons is difficult to capture. This is why the European Union Agency for Fundamental Rights (FRA) encourages the adoption of intersecting perspectives to describe age and ageing, covering physical, mental and social changes that occur as a person ages, while avoiding rigid definitions.[34]

On the other hand, referring to a metric age is essential when collecting data, making it easier to identify the problems and needs of older people, including migrants. The UN Independent Expert on the enjoyment of all human rights by older persons (the UN Independent Expert/IEOP) has pointed out difficulties with data collection that arise, among other things, from the relativity of age, the variety of circumstances, conditions, cultures and other considerations and factors, which are themselves subject to change. Therefore, in her report of 2019, the Independent Expert suggested

---

32 Statista, "Mortality and Life Expectancy Statistics: Life Expectancy by Continent and Gender 2022. Statista Research Centre 20 October 2022", https://ec.europa.eu/eurostat/statistics-explained/index.php?title=Mortality_and_life_expectancy_statistics.

33 Data from the World Bank, https://data.worldbank.org/indicator/SP.DYN.LE00.IN.

34 FRA, ed., *Shifting Perceptions: Towards a Rights-Based Approach to Ageing*, Focus / FRA, European Union Agency for Fundamental Rights (Luxembourg: Publications Office of the European Union, 2018), https://doi.org/10.2811/533946.

considering ageing as a social contextual construct, involving far more life-course factors and conditions than simply chronological or numerical age, such as biological and socioeconomic determinants, which are also subject to change (para. 22).[35]

During the COVID–19 pandemic, the Independent Expert, Claudia Mahler, expressed alarm that most countries only had fragmented information, if any at all, about the lived realities of older persons. This situation led to inequalities faced by older persons, who frequently remained invisible. As a result, decision-makers faced critical difficulties in defining an informed and successful public policy that is inclusive of the needs of older persons.[36] It is worth noting that it is not uncommon for statistics and reports to lump older migrants in together with migrants with disabilities, or other vulnerable groups, without looking at the specific needs of older people who have no disability. This approach can even be encountered in the 2021 UNHCR Global Report.[37]

In treaties and other international documents, descriptions of the notion of older persons are often limited to indicating the age threshold at which the working life ends. In European documents, older age tends to begin at the age of 65 years.[38] Meanwhile, regional treaties adopted on the American and African forums – the Inter-American Convention on Protecting the

35 Independent Expert, "Report of the Independent Expert on the Enjoyment of All Human Rights by Older Persons, Visit to Mozambique A/HRC/42/43/ADD.2" (Human Rights Council, 2019), 6, https://uhri.ohchr.org/en/document/ba0cd581-3c27-47c4-ae2b-67861c434ee7.

36 UN Independent Expert, "Impact of the Coronavirus Disease (COVID-19) on the Enjoyment of All Human Rights by Older Persons Report of the Independent Expert on the Enjoyment of All Human Rights by Older Persons, Claudia Mahler A/75/205", (General Assembly, 2020), https://undocs.org/A/75/205.

37 UNHCR, "Global Report. The Stories behind the Numbers" (Geneva, 2021), 161, https://reporting.unhcr.org/global-report-202.

38 For example, Committee of Ministers, "Recommendation CM/Rec(2014)2 Adopted by the Committee of Ministers of the Council of Europe on 19 February 2014", https://rm.coe.int/1680695bce; European Commission, "Green Paper on Ageing: Fostering Solidarity and Responsibility between Generations, 27 January 2021 COM(2021) 50 Final" (European Union, 2021), https://ec.europa.eu/info/sites/default/files/1_en_act_part1_v8_0.pdf.

Human Rights of Older Persons of 2015[39] and the Protocol to the African Charter on Human and Peoples' Rights on the Rights of Older Persons[40] – indicate a rigid age threshold of 60 years or above.

Migrants are also a very diverse group within themselves. International law does not contain a universally accepted definition of a "migrant." There are (at least) two approaches to defining "migrants." The *"residualist view"* perceives migrants as people who have moved from their usual residence for any reason *other than* fleeing war or persecution. Thus, according to this concept, migrants are people who are united by the feature of "not being refugees."[41] This view excludes war refugees and anyone who, as stipulated in Article 1 of the Geneva Convention Relating to the Status of Refugees, "owing to well-founded fear of being persecuted for reasons of race, religion, nationality, membership of a particular social group or political opinion, is outside the country of his nationality and is unable or, owing to such fear, is unwilling to avail himself of the protection of that country; or who, not having a nationality and being outside the country of his former habitual residence as a result of such events, is unable or, owing to such fear, is unwilling to return to it."[42]

Meanwhile, the *inclusivist view* holds that a migrant is anyone who has moved from their usual residence, regardless of their legal status and motivations for moving. In other words, migrants include refugees, foreign workers, trafficking victims, trailing spouses, international students and many more or less precise categories of individuals.

---

39 OAS, "Inter-American Convention on Protecting the Human Rights of Older Persons Adopted at the General Assembly of the Organization of American States in Washington, DC, on June 15, 2015", http://www.oas.org/en/sla/dil/docs/inter_american_treaties_A-70_human_rights_older_persons.pdf.

40 African Union, "Protocol to the African Charter on Human And Peoples' Rights on the Rights of Older Persons in Africa of 31 January 2016," https://au.int/en/treaties/protocol-african-charter-human-and-peoples-rights-rights-older-persons.

41 See more at https://meaningofmigrants.org/.

42 United Nations, "Convention Relating to the Status of Refugees, 28 July 1951", (UNTS vol 189, p. 137), https://treaties.un.org/pages/ViewDetailsII.aspx?src=TREATY&mtdsg_no=V-2&chapter=5&Temp=mtdsg2&clang=_en; UNTS, "Protocol Relating to the Status of Refugees No. 879, 606 UNTS 268", 1967.

This *inclusivist view is* presented by the International Organization for Migration (IOM). IOM's definition of "a migrant" covers various types of "persons on the move." According to its "Glossary on Migration", a "migrant" is: "an umbrella term, not defined under international law, reflecting the common lay understanding of a person who moves away from his or her place of usual residence, whether within a country or across an international border, temporarily or permanently, and for a variety of reasons. The term includes a number of well-defined legal categories of people, such as migrant workers; persons whose particular types of movements are legally defined, such as smuggled migrants; as well as those whose status or means of movement are not specifically defined under international law, such as international students."[43]

Thus, the IOM's inclusivist approach covers, among others, the most vulnerable migrants: asylum seekers, displaced persons, documented migrants, documented migrant workers, environmental migrants, expatriates, internal migrants, and internally displaced persons. The group of international migrants covers, for example: long-term migrants, migrants in a regular situation, migrants in an irregular situation, migrants in vulnerable situations, migrant workers, permanent residents, seasonal migrant workers, separated children, short-term migrants, smuggled migrants, victims of trafficking, undocumented migrants, undocumented migrant workers etc.

According to the United Nations High Commissioner for Refugees (UNHCR), the difference between a migrant and a refugee lies primarily in the fact that the migrant chooses to move, not because of an imminent threat to life or freedom, but to find a job, get an education, be reunited with family or for other personal reasons. Unlike refugees, migrants do not fear persecution or serious harm in their home countries, they continue to enjoy the protection of their governments and can return to their country of origin.[44]

However, in the contemporary world, mixed migrations prevail. People travel together, usually irregularly, along the same routes and using the

43 International Organization for Migration, *Glossary on Migration*, vol. 34, International Migration Law (Geneva, 2019), 132.

44 UN High Commissioner for Refugees, "The 10-Point Plan in Action, 2016 – Glossary, December 2016", https://www.refworld.org/docid/59e99eb94.html.

same means of transport, but for different reasons. It is also expected that the reasons for leaving a country are both economic and political.[45] That is why the international community, in the 2016 Declaration for Refugees and Migrants, confirmed states' obligations under international law to all people with special needs, including older persons, in vulnerable situations who are travelling within large movements of refugees and migrants.[46]

So, the broad understanding of a migrant is fully justified in this study. However, it appears reasonable, following the United Nations Department of Economic and Social Affairs, to exclude temporary movements that are due to recreation, holidays, visits to friends and relatives, business, medical treatment or religious pilgrimages.[47] Thus, these categories are not taken into account in this study. It refers to older migrants being voluntarily or forcibly "on the move" or aged in the host country.

45 International Organization for Migration, *Glossary on Migration*, 34:141.

46 UN General Assembly, "New Urban Agenda, Resolution Adopted by the General Assembly on 23 December 2016, A/RES/71/256", https://habitat3.org/wp-content/uploads/New-Urban-Agenda-GA-Adopted-68th-Plenary-N1646655-E.pdf.

47 UNDESA United Nations Statistic Division, "Recommendations on Statistics of International Migration, Revision 1," Series M, Statistical Papers No. 58' (United Nations, 1998), 9, para. 32, https://unstats.un.org/unsd/publication/seriesm/seriesm_58rev1e.pdf.

2. Older migrants and the various faces of vulnerability

2.1. Attempts at conceptualisation

The vulnerability of older adults is undoubtedly a great challenge for states and their social systems, as well as for civil society and older people themselves.[48] Martha Fineman[49] and Kieran Walsh and colleagues write about vulnerability in old age coinciding with the loss of choice, possibilities and social exclusion.[50] However, as Jonathan Herring argues, vulnerability is a vague term used in many disciplines, including law and politics. It may refer to a person who needs special attention, who may not participate in certain activities, or to a group that is entitled to protection. He also notes that everyone is vulnerable in certain circumstances.[51] Indeed, old age and migratory status may become such circumstances separately, but when experienced together they intensify human vulnerability. Older migrants are certainly at higher risk of being subjected to discriminatory practices, violence, exclusion, various social disadvantages, or economic hardship than other groups within a state, particularly during a period of conflict, crisis or disaster. They often face discrimination based on two or more grounds simultaneously (e.g. age, race, nationality, gender, disability or religion)

48 Martha Albertson Fineman, "'Elderly' as Vulnerable: Rethinking the Nature of Individual and Societal Responsibility", *SSRN Electronic Journal*, 2012, 110, https://doi.org/10.2139/ssrn.2088159.

49 Fineman, "'Elderly' as Vulnerable".

50 RosNET, "Multidimensional Social Exclusion in Later Life: Briefing Paper and a Roadmap for Future Collaborations in Research and Policy", in *K. Walsh and T. Scharf (Series Eds.), ROSEnet Briefing Paper Series: No. 6. CA 15122 Reducing Old-Age Exclusion: Collaborations in Research and Policy*, 2020, http://rosenetcost.com/wp-content/uploads/2017/01/cost_rosenet_actionpolicy6_web.pdf; Kieran Walsh, Thomas Scharf, and Norah Keating, "Social Exclusion of Older Persons: A Scoping Review and Conceptual Framework", *European Journal of Ageing* 14, No. 1 (March 2017): 93, https://doi.org/10.1007/s10433-016-0398-8.

51 Jonathan Herring, *Older People in Law and Society* (Oxford: Oxford University Press, 2009), 6–7.

as well as intersectional discrimination emerging from the interaction of grounds of discrimination resulting in a new type of discrimination.[52] In particular, racism combined with ageism affects all spheres of migrants' lives, including their mental and physical condition.[53]

However, not all migrants, even older migrants, should be considered vulnerable and older migrants' rights are not always violated. Their vulnerability to human rights violations depends on their legal status, level of integration, age and the circumstances of leaving their country of origin and current place of residence.[54] For example, in the European Union, the legal situation of the older EU citizens enjoying the freedom of movement and the older third-country nationals differs significantly. In yet another situation are those seeking international protection in EU Member States.

The European Union Agency for Asylum (EUAA) notes that the Common European Asylum System (CEAS) instruments use different concepts, such as "vulnerability," "special needs," "special reception needs" or "special procedural guarantees."[55] Article 2(d) of the Directive 2013/32/EU of the European Parliament and of the Council of 26 June 2013 on common procedures for granting and withdrawing international protection (recast) provides the definition of "applicant in need of special procedural guarantees" as meaning "an applicant whose ability to benefit from the rights and comply with the obligations provided for in this Directive is limited due to individual circumstances."[56] Article 2(k) of the Directive 2013/33/EU Laying down Standards for the Reception of Applicants for

52 Sandra Fredman, *Intersectional discrimination in EU gender equality and non-discrimination law.* (LU: Publications Office, 2016), 51, https://data.europa.eu/doi/10.2838/241520.

53 See more: Sue Westwood, ed., *Ageing, Diversity and Equality*, Routledge Advances in Sociology (London: Routledge, 2019); Robert Joseph Taylor, "Race and Mental Health Among Older Adults: Within- and Between-Group Comparisons", *Innovation in Aging* 4, No. 5 (1 September 2020): igaa056, https://doi.org/10.1093/geroni/igaa056.

54 Dolberg, Sigurđardóttir, and Trummer, "Ageism and Older Immigrants", 180.

55 European Union Agency for Asylum., *Guidance on Vulnerability in Asylum and Reception: Operational Standards and Indicators.* (LU: Publications Office, 2024), p. 20, https://data.europa.eu/doi/10.2847/110546

56 O. J. L 180, 29/06/2013, pp. 60–95, https://eur-lex.europa.eu/legal-content/en/TXT/?uri=celex%3A32013L0032

International Protection (recast) defines an "applicant with special reception needs" as "a vulnerable person, in accordance with Article 21, who is in need of special guarantees in order to benefit from the rights and comply with the obligations provided for in this Directive."[57]

The EUAA, describing the vulnerability of asylum seekers refers to the European Court of Human Rights (ECtHR) in its landmark case *M.S.S. v Belgium and Greece*[58], where the Grand Chamber found that the applicant, an asylum seeker, was "particularly vulnerable because of everything he had been through during his migration and the traumatic experiences he was likely to have endured previously."[59] In the ECtHR opinion, the vulnerability is inherent in the situation of asylum seekers, who are members of a particularly underprivileged and vulnerable population group in need of special protection.

The EUAA, following UNHCR and the International Detention Coalition's Vulnerability Screening Tool, also explains that "vulnerability is not a permanent or fixed feature; it can change over time. A situation of vulnerability of an applicant for international protection can be shaped by various factors that may be related to both individual characteristics (such as age) or to external factors, which may coexist and intersect with each other."[60]

So what is meant by the vulnerability of older migrants? As Katarzyna Gałka noted, the European Court of Human Rights, when considering asylum cases, "does not provide an abstract definition of vulnerability in its jurisprudence, and the content of the concept must be decoded on

57 O. J. L 180/96 29.6.2013, pp. 96–116, 2013, https://eur-lex.europa.eu/legal-content/EN/TXT/?uri=CELEX:32019L0882.

58 European Court of Human Rights, "*M.S.S. v Belgium and Greece*", Application No. 30696/09, Judgement 21 January 2011 (Grand Chamber)," https://hudoc.echr.coe.int/fre#{%22itemid%22:[%22001-103050 %22]}

59 Para. 232.

60 European Union Agency for Asylum (2024), p. 20; UNHCR and IDC, *Vulnerability Screening Tool – Identifying and addressing vulnerability: a tool for asylum and migration systems*, 2016, p. 2, https://www.refworld.org/policy/opguidance/unhcr/2016/en/112752; UNHCR, "Age, Gender and Diversity (AGD) and Intersectionality", 2023, https://www.unhcr.org/age-gender-diversity/.

a case-by-case basis."[61] The ECtHR assesses the vulnerability of foreign asylum seekers firstly in terms of their vulnerability resulting from the harrowing experiences that have led such people to flee their homeland, and secondly with waiting for a decision to grant international protection. In some cases, complex vulnerability and human rights violations result from the state's failure to act, e.g. by not issuing a decision within a reasonable period. The court considers vulnerability not only related to the applicant's status for international protection but also to belonging to another category of persons needing special protection, such as children or single mothers with young children.[62] Therefore, the ECtHR's identification of the vulnerability of older asylum seekers in the future cannot be excluded.

Meanwhile, according to the International Organization for Migration, vulnerability within a migration context has been defined as "the limited capacity to avoid, resist, cope with, or recover from harm. This limited capacity is the result of the unique interaction of individual, household, community, and structural characteristics and conditions."[63]

The concept of "migrants in vulnerable situations" is described in the key Report of the United Nations High Commissioner for Human Rights (UNHCHR) entitled "Principles and practical guidance on the protection of the human rights of migrants in vulnerable situations."[64] They are defined as those who "are unable effectively to enjoy their human rights, are at increased risk of violations and abuse and who, accordingly, are entitled to call on a duty bearer's heightened duty of care" (para. 12). The

---

61 Katarzyna Gałka, "Vulnerability and Its Implications: Some Comments in the Light of the Strasbourg Case Law Concerning Asylum Seekers", *Espaço Jurídico Journal of Law [EJJL]* 22, no. 2 (22 December 2021): 287, https://doi.org/10.18593/ejjl.29950.

62 Katarzyna Gałka, "Status and Protection of Applicants for International Protection in the European Union with Special Needs as Regards Reception Conditions", in *Human Rights in the European Paradigm of the Protection of Aliens*, ed. Elżbieta Karska et al. (Warsaw, 2023), 384.

63 International Organization for Migration, *Glossary on Migration*, 34:227.

64 UN OHCHR and Global Migration Group, *Principles and Practical Guidance on the Protection of the Human Rights of Migrants in Vulnerable Situations. Report of the United Nations High Commissioner for Human Rights, 3 January 2018, A/HRC/37/34* (Geneva, 2018), https://ap.ohchr.org/documents/dpage_e.aspx?si=A%2FHRC%2F37%2F34.

report indicates the complexity of vulnerability of migrants: "the vulnerable situations that migrants face can arise from a range of factors that may intersect or coexist simultaneously, influencing and exacerbating each other and also evolving or changing over time as circumstances change."[65]

Moreover, the UNHCHR describes their vulnerability to human rights violations: "vulnerability to human rights violations is the result of multiple and intersecting forms of discrimination, inequality and structural and societal dynamics that lead to diminished and unequal levels of power and enjoyment of rights. As a matter of principle, and in order to ensure that every migrant is able to access appropriate protection of their rights, the situation of each person must be assessed individually" (para. 13).[66]

Elena Pariotti notes that "the notion of vulnerability seems to have a specific potential in human rights discourse and practice: It may support an understanding of the overall impact of human rights in terms that are more comprehensive compared to the most diffused and traditional view. If this latter looks at human rights mainly or exclusively as a means to protect against power, maintaining that human rights have the aim of protecting the vulnerable leads to taking into consideration a condition that is much more diffused and multiform and that has to do with dominance. In other terms, the reference to vulnerability may enlarge the sphere of relevance of human rights language for the human condition."[67]

2.2. An inexhaustible list of vulnerabilities

The Special Rapporteur on the human rights of migrants refers directly to the situation of older migrants, arguing that migration in later life can be particularly traumatic, because of the severed social ties and lack of facilities, rights and protection in unfamiliar new environments.[68] On the other

---

65 UN OHCHR and Global Migration Group, 5.

66 UN OHCHR and Global Migration Group, 6.

67 Elena Pariotti, "Vulnerability and Human Rights: Which Compatibility?", *International Journal for the Semiotics of Law – Revue Internationale de Sémiotique Juridique* 36, No. 4 (August 2023): 1402, https://doi.org/10.1007/s11196-023-09977-y.

68 Special Rapporteur on the human rights of migrants, "Report of the Special Rapporteur on the Human Rights of Migrants, Felipe González Morales, 19 July 2022, A/77/189" (United Nations General Assembly, 2022), para. 61,

hand, ageing outside the home country entails many integration problems and obstacles in access to healthcare and social services[69] as people who have worked and spent many years in a foreign country sometimes remain outside of mainstream society. In general, regardless of the moment of migration, older migrants are often exposed to various types of inequality, discrimination and violations of their human rights.

The Special Rapporteur on the human rights of migrants argues, for example, that migrant workers face difficulties in accessing social protection systems designed for nationals and citizens, including pensions. He also notes that:

> "Migrant workers face difficulties in accessing social protection systems designed for nationals and citizens, including pensions, social security and employment benefits, as well as parental, childcare and elderly care benefits owing to eligibility (often permanent residency requirements), cost and time constraints, limitations in portability and transferability of benefits, as well as owing to a lack of information and language barriers in countries of origin, transit and destination. Migrant workers are often excluded from social protection systems, and they are therefore especially vulnerable to economic shocks, unemployment and poverty, as they often do not enjoy the same rights and protection as nationals. Even if eligible, migrant workers face barriers in accessing unemployment insurance, parental and sick leaves, as well as disability insurance, pensions and other benefits, even though they may pay into these systems. At the same time, they risk losing entitlement to any existent social security benefits in their countries of origin owing to extended periods living abroad."[70]

Reports and research also show that migrants, including older migrants, are increasingly the targets of racist violence and hate speech, as well as facing

https://documents-dds-ny.un.org/doc/UNDOC/GEN/N22/431/49/PDF/N2243149.pdf?OpenElement.

69 Véronique Griner-Abraham, "[Growing old in exile: a double punishment or a double luck?]", *Soins. Psychiatrie*, No. 293 (2014): 37–43.

70 Special Rapporteur on the human rights of migrants, "Report of the Special Rapporteur on the Human Rights of Migrants, Felipe González Morales, Protection of the Labour and Human Rights of Migrant Workers", (United Nations General Assembly, 2023), para. 43, https://documents-dds-ny.un.org/doc/UNDOC/GEN/N23/207/02/PDF/N2320702.pdf?OpenElement.

discriminatory policies and attitudes hindering their access to the labour market and services in healthcare.[71]

This all means that the vulnerability of older migrants is as diverse as the migrants and older people themselves. For this reason, it is impossible to itemise all the older migrants' vulnerabilities, because everyone is vulnerable in certain circumstances. Recalling certain situations described in the scholarship and international reports can, at most, shed some light on the situation of different groups of older migrants. With this in mind, a few of the "vulnerable situations" faced by voluntary and forced migrants will be referenced here. However, many phenomena and situations affect both groups equally, such as racial discrimination, ageism and global threats, including the COVID-19 pandemic. Older persons become particularly vulnerable when participating in migrations arising from gross human rights violations and wars. The Independent Expert on the enjoyment of all human rights by older persons, the United Nations High Commissioner for Human Rights, the UN High Commissioner for Refugees,[72] the Open-Ended Working Group on Ageing (OEWGA) and the World Health Organization (WHO) all point out the formal and informal barriers in enjoining the human rights by older refugees, war refugees, displaced persons and asylum seekers in emergencies. They indicate discriminatory immigration policies, economic difficulties, language barriers, a lack of awareness of available services, structural constraints, the inadequacy of provisional shelters, cultural differences, etc. At the same time, these international bodies report on gaps in data collection on older persons.[73] Non-governmental organisations also reported that sex- and age-disaggregated data is rarely collected,

---

71 For example European Network Against Racism, "Racism and Discrimination in Europe in the Context of the Migration in Europe. ENAR Shadow Report 2015–2016" (Brussels, 2017), https://www.enar-eu.org/wp-content/uploads/shadowreport_2015x2016_long_low_res.pdf; Mia Pattillo et al., "Racism against Racialized Migrants in Healthcare in Europe: A Scoping Review", *International Journal for Equity in Health* 22, No. 1 (29 September 2023): 201, https://doi.org/10.1186/s12939-023-02014-1.

72 UNHCR, "UNHCR's Policy on Older Refugees (UNHCR, 19 April 2000), EC/50/SC/CRP.1."

73 Independent Expert, "Report of the Independent Expert on the Enjoyment of All Human Rights by Older Persons, Visit to Mozambique A/HRC/42/43/ADD.2".

contributing to the invisibility whereby older people are consistently neglected in humanitarian operations and policy.[74]

The UNHCHR report is accompanied by "Principles and Guidelines, supported by practical guidance, on the human rights protection of migrants in vulnerable situations" which focus mainly on vulnerable situations associated with the reasons for leaving the country of origin, situations that migrants encounter during their journey and at destination and with a person's identity, condition or circumstances. These "Principles and Guidelines..." are not dedicated to older migrants, but concern all potentially vulnerable categories of migrants, which includes older persons. Older migrants are mentioned in the context of the guideline for border guards to take all reasonable measures to minimise the time during which migrants are delayed at borders or other crossing points on their journey and to provide proper humanitarian assistance during border procedures and delays, such as the provision of shelter, gender-responsive water and sanitation facilities, medical care, including sexual and reproductive health services and culturally appropriate food. Moreover, states and their authorities should avoid the immigration detention of people who have specific needs or who are particularly at risk of exploitation, abuse, sexual or gender-based violence, or other forms of violence. Finally, state authorities should take measures to ensure that migrants enjoy a proper standard of living for migrants in temporary locations (e.g. refugee camps). Such facilities should be accessible to all migrants, including older persons. An adequate standard of living covers, among other things, safe food sufficient in quantity and quality to satisfy an individual's dietary needs, safe drinking water and culturally acceptable sanitation, adequate and appropriate clothing, adequate housing and the continuous improvement of living conditions.[75]

---

74 Jo Wells, "The Neglected Generation the Impact of Displacement on Older People" (HelpAge International, 2013), 5, https://www.refworld.org/docid/524571814.html.

75 UN OHCHR and Global Migration Group, *Principles and Practical Guidance on the Protection of the Human Rights of Migrants in Vulnerable Situations. Report of the United Nations High Commissioner for Human Rights, 3 January 2018, A/HRC/37/34.*

The "Principles and Guidelines..." draw attention to crucial situations whereby, while seeking international protection, older persons may be deprived of their fundamental human rights, such as the right to health, food, shelter, etc.

However, it should be remembered that, while in exile, they also face other problems. The research shows that older refugees and war refugees are particularly vulnerable to psychosocial problems, as they are often socially and physically separated from their families and communities. On the other hand, as their contribution to survival can be limited, they may experience the loss of social and family support and respect and the diminishing of their self-esteem. They may be recognised as a burden on surviving family members and communities. It happens that older people are often left behind when the rest of their community has been displaced.[76]

The UNHCR Emergency Handbook of 2020 indicates that older persons who are forced to leave their country or place of residence are at particular risk of violence, sexual and domestic abuse and exploitation by family members and others. They are more likely to be excluded from access to humanitarian assistance, education, livelihoods, healthcare, and other services. These risks are compounded for women, persons with disabilities and older LGBTI persons.[77]

HelpAge International identified several other issues facing older people in displacement, such as the lack of access to information about their rights and available legal services and mobility, or even the confidence to seek advice, as well as barriers to achieving a legal status that would allow them to benefit from services, schemes and entitlements. On the other hand, the lack of knowledge about older people's rights and needs among international agencies, refugee response administrations and civil society was identified.[78]

---

76 Karlsson and Jönsson, "Forced Migration, Older Refugees and Displacement", 214.

77 UNHCR, "Emergency Handbook. Older Persons", 2020, 3, https://emergency.unhcr.org/protection/persons-risk/older-persons#_ga=2.195038444.1980655889.1684257370-604704032.1684257370.

78 Veronique Barbelet, "Older People in Displacement Falling through the Cracks of Emergency Responses" (London: HelpAge International, Humanitarian Policy Group, Overseas Development Institute, 2018), 1.

Other aspects of older migrants' vulnerability were taken up by the UN Secretary-General in his report of 2011 when he noted that some societies left older people behind when coping with large migratory movements and indicated violence against them that arose from traditional beliefs and accusations of sorcery, as well as their difficult situation.[79]

Armed conflicts make older persons particularly vulnerable, both those who remain in their homes and those who become war refugees or internally displaced persons. HelpAge International, referring to this humanitarian crisis, notes that: "...while war does not discriminate, the international response does. Time and again, the toll of war on older people is overlooked as they struggle to survive and piece together a new normal."[80]

In this context, particular attention should be paid to older persons experiencing the war in Ukraine. Due to the demographic structure of Ukraine, with a high rate of older persons (especially women), this war has been called the "oldest humanitarian crisis in the world."[81] The Special Rapporteur on the rights of persons with disabilities – Gerard Quinn – together with the Independent Expert on the enjoyment of all human rights by older persons – Claudia Mahler –noted that: "persons with disabilities and older persons during armed conflict are often left behind because of a lack of consideration of their particular needs, leading in many cases to abandonment."[82]

Another aspect of vulnerability is tied to climate change, which has a severe effect on the older population, with its impacts magnified by ageism,

---

79 UN Secretary General, "Follow-up to the Second World Assembly on Ageing Report of the Secretary-General, 22 July 2011, A/66/173." (United Nations General Assembly, 2011), paras 12 and 15, https://www.un.org/development/desa/ageing/resources/general-assembly-reports.html.

80 HelpAge International, "The Impact of War on Older People (in Ukraine and Everywhere Else)", https://www.helpage.org, 13 April 2022, https://www.helpage.org/newsroom/latest-news/the-impact-of-war-on-older-people-in-ukraine-and-everywhere-else/.

81 Age Platform Europe, "Ukraine: The 'Oldest' Humanitarian Crisis in the World, 15 March 2022", https://www.age-platform.eu/special-briefing/ukraine-%E2%80%98oldest%E2%80%99-humanitarian-crisis-world.

82 See at the UN HCHR website: https://www.ohchr.org/en/press-releases/2022/03/ukraine-aged-and-those-disabilities-face-heightened-risks-say-un-experts.

poverty and social exclusion. In its "Analytical study on the promotion and protection of the rights of older persons in the context of climate change," the UNHCHR stressed that: "the climate change effects can impair the realisation of older persons' rights to life, health, food, water and sanitation, housing, freedom of movement, livelihoods, social protection, development and culture, among others. These impacts can be magnified by multiple and intersecting forms of discrimination, including on the basis of gender, race and ethnicity, disability, and migration status."[83]

The situation worsens when an older person becomes a climate migrant. The Special Rapporteur on the promotion and protection of human rights in the context of climate change, in addressing the issue of ensuring the legal capacity to protect the human rights of people displaced across international borders due to climate change, recognises age as a characteristic that may contribute to additional risks when crossing international borders as a result of climate displacement.[84]

After the ECtHR's ruling in the *Verein KlimaSeniorinnen Schweiz and Others v. Switzerland*[85] case, no one today can question climate change's

83 UN Secretary General, "Analytical Study on the Promotion and Protection of the Rights of Older Persons in the Context of Climate Change Report of the Office of the United Nations High Commissioner for Human Rights, 30 April 2021, A/HRC/47/46", 2021., para. 64.

84 UN Secretary General, "Report of the Special Rapporteur on the Promotion and Protection of Human Rights in the Context of Climate Change Promotion and Protection of Human Rights in the Context of Climate Change Mitigation, Loss and Damage and Participation, 22 July 2022, A/77/226.", https://documents-dds-ny.un.org/doc/UNDOC/GEN/N22/438/51/PDF/N2243851.pdf?OpenElement.

85 European Court of Human Rights (Grand Chamber), "*Verein KlimaSeniorinnen Schweiz and Others v. Switzerland*, Application No. 53600/20; Judgement 9 April 2024", https://hudoc.echr.coe.int/eng#{%22itemid%22:[%22002-13649 %22]}. In this case, the association represented over 2500 senior women from Switzerland, who complained that their age and gender made them particularly vulnerable to the effects of heatwaves linked to climate change. Before the ECtHR, the applicants alleged that the Swiss Government had taken insufficient climate change mitigation action and failed to comply with its positive obligations to effectively protect their lives and respect private and family life. The ECtHR held that Article 8 of the ECHR (respect private and family life) encompasses a right for state authorities to effectively protect themselves from

impact on older people's lives and rights. The case illustrates the vulnerability of older women in the face of rising temperatures. The plaintiff organisation in the case represented older women living in one of the wealthiest countries in the world. One should be aware, therefore, of the multiplying severity of climate change for older people coming from countries of the Global South affected not only by climate change but also by various conflicts, including conflicts over access to water.

Like war refugees, older people displaced by climate change tend to live in inadequate conditions – in camps or informal settlements – without access to basic services and in conditions conducive to various types of disease. Challenges in supporting them are undoubtedly poor support systems and difficulties in accessing telecommunications and information, sometimes due to language and cultural barriers. The Independent Expert notes that older people are at an increased risk of violence, exploitation and abuse, which are compounded by barriers to accessing humanitarian assistance and essential services. At the same time, older people are often overlooked in programmes targeting internally displaced persons and refugees.[86]

The COVID-19 pandemic is another example of circumstances that increase the vulnerability of older migrants to the failure to exercise their human rights, both those "on the move" and those already settled in countries that have received them. UNHCR and HelpAge International reported, for instance, that the COVID-19 pandemic limited older displaced people's access to vital rights and services, while also decreasing contact with their families and community activities.[87] The pandemic intensified

---

the serious adverse effects of climate change on lives, health, well-being, and quality of life.

86 UN Secretary General, "Report of the Independent Expert on the Enjoyment of All Human Rights, Claudia Malher, 23 July, Human Rights of Older Persons in the Context of Climate Change-Induced Disasters, 25 July 2023 A/78/226" (United Nations General Assembly, 2023), para. 29, https://www.ohchr.org/en/documents/thematic-reports/a78226-human-rights-older-persons-context-climate-change-induced.

87 HelpAge International, "Older Refugees at Heightened Risk of Exclusion as COVID-19 Continues to Strike the Americas", HelpAge International, 2021, https://www.helpage.org/news/older-refugees-at-heightened-risk-of-exclusion-as-covid19-continues-to-strike-the-americas/.

their loneliness, anxiety and depression, deepening pre-existing physical and mental health vulnerabilities as well as environmental, social, cultural-specific, economic and welfare factors.[88]

The vulnerability of older migrants "on the move" consists not only of the trauma, often coming after torture, of the hardship of the journey, but also of the temporary nature of their situation related to the asylum procedures (often incomprehensible), waiting to be transferred to another country due to European asylum rules, or waiting for a residence permit. The EUAA, in relation to the asylum procedures, notes that "applicants in a vulnerable situation may experience barriers to effectively access this information (e.g. illiteracy, hearing impairments, vision impairments, etc.). They may need to receive relevant content adapted to and targeting their special needs to ensure that adequate support is provided (e.g. attestation of medical documentation, support to victims of gender-based violence (GBV), etc.)"[89]

Finally, older persons may also be stateless and without any chance of obtaining citizenship, which entails exclusion in almost all spheres of life. Some older migrants cannot pass language and other tests as a condition for naturalisation.[90] Quite often, the refugee's life in a host country brings disappointment as they face discrimination and other stresses in their new home country.[91]

---

88 Ghassan El Tatary and Neeraj Gill, "The Impact of the COVID-19 Pandemic on the Mental Health and Wellbeing of Refugees and Asylum Seekers-A Narrative Review of the Literature", *Australasian Psychiatry* 30, No. 6 (December 2022): 729, https://doi.org/10.1177/10398562221131154; Souraya Sidani et al., "Social Isolation and Loneliness in Older Immigrants during COVID-19: A Scoping Review", *International Journal of Migration, Health and Social Care* 18, No. 2 (31 May 2022): 164–78, https://doi.org/10.1108/IJMHSC-08-2021-0071.

89 European Union Agency for Asyum (2024), p. 25.

90 UN Secretary General, "Report of the Independent Expert on the Enjoyment of All Human Rights, Claudia Malher, Human Rights of Older Persons in the Context of Climate Change-Induced Disasters, 25 July 2023 A/78/226", para. 17.

91 Mulki Mölsä et al., "Mental Health among Older Refugees: The Role of Trauma, Discrimination, and Religiousness", *Aging & Mental Health* 21, No. 8 (3 August 2017): 829–37, https://doi.org/10.1080/13607863.2016.1165183.

In many cases, long-established foreigners who have grown old in their host country, regardless of status, remain outside the social mainstream anyway. They are often overlooked in terms of public and social policy discussions on ageing.[92] In many countries, members of migrant communities tend to be more likely than other members of society to be unable to live independently in old age due to disability.[93] Older women from various migrant groups often face barriers when accessing social and health services due to their lower literacy, including health literacy, disempowerment and language barriers.[94] For example, a review of various research shows that ageism and cultural differences are a key determinant of health that negatively affects older Syrian refugees' physical and mental health, as well as their access to social support and healthcare.[95] Another example of vulnerability is the situation of Arab women, who may be at heightened risk of negative mental health outcomes due to separation from long-intact family systems and community networks and increased isolation upon resettlement.[96] The research shows that older migrants are, on average, more likely to be lonely than older adults who have not migrated.[97] The loneliness and lack of contact with relatives of older migrants, often resulting in psychological problems, could be reduced through new technologies, but older migrants' use of digital technology remains very low. This lack of digital

92 Matt Flynn et al., "Editorial: Ageing and Migration Status: Intersectional Forms of Discrimination and Exclusion", *Frontiers in Psychology* 14 (21 February 2023): 2, https://doi.org/10.3389/fpsyg.2023.1150578.
93 Zeinab Majid et al., "Global Frailty: The Role of Ethnicity, Migration and Socioeconomic Factors", *Maturitas* 139 (September 2020): 34, https://doi.org/10.1016/j.maturitas.2020.05.010.
94 Reid et al., "Frailty in Ethnic Minority Women", 29.
95 Maya Abi Chahine and Hanna Kienzler, "Ageism, an Invisible Social Determinant of Health for Older Syrian Refugees in Lebanon: A Service Providers' Perspective", *Conflict and Health* 16, No. 1 (24 November 2022): 11, https://doi.org/10.1186/s13031-022-00491-9.
96 Nashwan, Cummings, and Gagnon, "Older Female Iraqi Refugees in the United States", 654.
97 Tineke Fokkema and Ruxandra Oana Ciobanu, "Older Migrants and Loneliness: Scanning the Field and Looking Forward", *European Journal of Ageing* 18, No. 3 (September 2021): 291, https://doi.org/10.1007/s10433-021-00646-2.

literacy deprives them of communication opportunities and potentially increases social support. Therefore, there is a need to help older migrants build new social networks in their new communities through measures such as language and digital education.[98] It is worth mentioning here that the loneliness of older migrants and the lack of care from the family remaining in the country of origin is only one side of the coin. The other is the barriers to family reunification for naturalised citizens and their elderly parents (usually mothers). Many European countries restrict family reunification policies, assuming that such migrants represent a future economic burden for ageing societies.[99]

Yet another factor influencing the vulnerability of older migrants is poverty. Migrants arriving at an older age in the host country, especially the involuntary ones, did not have opportunities to prepare for old age, and those who arrived in their youth are often excluded from social security schemes.[100] Often, therefore, they cannot count on pensions or, in some countries, they may receive only social pensions. Migrant women, who have spent their lives caring for family members or taking up informal work, are usually in a worse situation.

Irregular migrants at risk of deportation can be placed in a vulnerable position in the host country's labour market. They are offered lower wages and sub-standard working conditions.[101]

Finally, vulnerable migrants may also include those for whom no one would suspect suffer from any problems. New vulnerabilities appear even

---

98 Prince Chiagozie Ekoh et al., "Forced Migration-Induced Diminished Social Networks and Support, and Its Impact on the Emotional Wellbeing of Older Refugees in Western Countries: A Scoping Review", *Archives of Gerontology and Geriatrics* 105 (February 2023): 6, https://doi.org/10.1016/j.archger.2022.104839.

99 Askola, "(No) Migrating for Family Care in Later Life".

100 Cruz-Martínez, "Rethinking Universalism", 40.

101 Clare Fox-Ruhs and Martin Ruhs, "The Fundamental Rights of Irregular Migrant Workers in the EU" (European Parliamnet, Policy Department for Citizens' Rights and Constitutional Affairs European Parliament, 2022), 57, https://www.europarl.europa.eu/RegData/etudes/STUD/2022/702670/IPOL_STU(2022)702670_EN.pdf.

in the case of those "lifestyle migrants"[102] who have decided to move from one to another EU state after retirement.[103] They may face loneliness (mostly after the death of a spouse),[104] various barriers to integration[105] or restrictions on participating in the public life of the community they have joined, such as not being able to participate in local elections in their chosen location. Older migrants may also face problems accessing benefits and healthcare, as well as with transferring pensions across borders.

The ILO's report identifies the two types of barriers faced by migrants – those relating to the legal framework (e.g. principle of nationality and territoriality) of the host or origin country, and those practical, arising in the effective enjoyment of their rights.[106] On the other hand, similar barriers may be experienced by those older persons who decide, after many years, to return to their country of origin after retirement in another country. Their reintegration into their country of origin does not always run smoothly.

102 Caroline Oliver, "Lifestyle Migration", in *Global Migration Governance*, ed. Alexander Betts (Oxford University Press, 2011), 133–52, https://doi.org/10.1093/acprof:oso/9780199600458.003.0006.

103 Marion Repetti, Christopher Phillipson, and Toni Calasanti, "Retirement Migration in Europe: A Choice for a Better Life?", *Sociological Research Online* 23, No. 4 (December 2018): 780–94, https://doi.org/10.1177/1360780418782243.

104 Dora Sampaio, "A Place to Grow Older … Alone? Living and Ageing as a Single Older Lifestyle Migrant in the Azores", *Area* 50, No. 4 (December 2018): 459–66, https://doi.org/10.1111/area.12414.

105 Jun Nagatomo, *Migration as Transnational Leisure: The Japanese Lifestyle Migrants in Australia*, Social Sciences in Asia 38 (Leiden ; Boston: Brill, 2014), 279.

106 *Extending Social Protection to Migrant Workers, Refugees and Their Families: A Guide for Policymakers and Practitioners* (Genève: International Labour Organisation (ILO), 2021), 30.

3. The starting point: Non-discrimination and the triad of obligations

3.1. Universal pillars

An awareness of older migrants' vulnerabilities allows us to extract, from the entire catalogue of human rights, those fundamental to their dignity and affecting the enjoyment of other rights. This brief and selective overview of vulnerabilities shows that, apart from the apparent right to life, many other older persons' rights in migratory situations may be at risk. The list is long and contains freedom from racial and age discrimination, freedom from torture, the right to seek asylum, to be free to leave any country, the right to citizenship, respect for family life, to information and learning, including digital learning, the right to an adequate standard of living, freedom from poverty, the right to adequate housing, employment and social security and the right to health. This list of rights of various natures, belonging to civil and social rights, is certainly incomplete.

As stipulated in the UDHR and the human rights treaties, states are under an obligation to respect, protect and fulfil each of these rights. "Respect" means that a state should refrain from interfering with the enjoyment of human rights. "Protect" involves the state's undertaking to ensure there are no human rights abuses by non-state actors. Finally, "fulfil" requires states to take positive action to facilitate the enjoyment of rights. Failing to perform one of these three obligations violates these rights. This triad of obligations runs across the divisions of rights (civil/social), meaning that states have both "negative obligations" (to refrain from violations of human rights) and "positive obligations" (to take steps to make the rights real).[107] Indeed, taking steps is crucial for mitigating older migrants' vulnerability

107 Marthe Fredvang and Simon Biggs, "The Rights of Older Persons. Protection and Gaps under Human Rights Law", Social Policy Working Paper (Brotherhood of St Laurence: Brotherhood of St Laurence, Centre for Public Policy, 2012), 9, https://library.bsl.org.au/jspui/bitstream/1/3179/1/Rights_of_older_persons_MFredvang&SBiggs_2012.pdf.

and safeguarding their "right to have rights"[108] regardless of their age, race, nationality and immigration status.

Therefore, any consideration about protecting older migrants under international law should start with protecting them against discrimination. Indeed, it can be assumed that if a category of vulnerable persons is overlooked in the context of discrimination, that situation will affect their enjoyment of all other human rights.

Certainly, not every distinction or difference in treatment can be called discrimination. From the nature of the status of citizen and non-citizen, there are differences in the enjoyment of certain human rights. Even the ICCPR contains rights dedicated exclusively to citizens (Article 25 – the right to participate in public affairs, vote, and access public services) and rights dedicated exclusively to migrants. Article 13 states that "an alien lawfully in the territory of a State Party to the present Covenant may be expelled therefrom only in pursuance of a decision reached in accordance with law and shall, except where compelling reasons of national security otherwise require, be allowed to submit the reasons against his expulsion and to have his case reviewed by, and be represented for the purpose before, the competent authority or a person or persons especially designated by the competent authority."

However, knowing the various vulnerabilities of older migrants, it is not the right to vote or to access public functions that matter most to them. Usually, in their case, such rights are simply meant to protect a dignified life/survival. On the other hand, an essential element of their protection is the right to be heard/consulted on issues that affect them. In this respect, they are neglected when constructing migration policies compared to younger migrants. Thus, not only do they have to face inequalities as older migrants and non-nationals, but they are also left behind within the migrant group. At the same time, like other categories of older persons in every corner of the world, older migrants face ageism. The World Health Organization, in its report of 2021, identified three dimensions of ageism – stereotypes, prejudice and discrimination. Each of these relates to

108 Melissa Stewart, " 'A New Law on Earth' Hannah Arendt and the Vision for a Positive Legal Framework to Guarantee the Right to Have Rights", *SSRN Electronic Journal*, 2021, 118, https://doi.org/10.2139/ssrn.3791785.

a distinct psychological faculty: thoughts (stereotypes), feelings (prejudices) and actions or behaviours (discrimination).[109] The law usually has limited possibilities to counteract human thoughts and feelings, but reacts to cases of age discrimination and aims to prevent people from carrying out these acts.[110]

Thus, the obligation of states in the area of non-discrimination is not only to refrain from adopting discriminatory laws or taking such measures but also to protect them from various types of discrimination by third parties and to take measures to ensure the non-discrimination requirement.

The interpretation of states' obligations in the area of non-discrimination under the ICCPR is a model that also applies when interpreting states' obligations arising from other universal treaties. It is of particular importance in the situation when there are no universal binding instruments protecting older persons' rights.

The ICCPR's preamble itself points to the need to take positive action to achieve the rights enshrined in the treaty: "recognizing that, in accordance with the Universal Declaration of Human Rights, the ideal of free human beings enjoying civil and political freedom and freedom from fear and want can only be achieved if conditions are created whereby everyone may enjoy his civil and political rights, as well as his economic, social and cultural rights."

Article 2 of the ICCPR sets out another obligation to undertake the necessary steps to achieve the rights recognised in the covenant in which it is contained:

> "1. Each State Party to the present Covenant undertakes to respect and to ensure to all individuals within its territory and subject to its jurisdiction the rights recognized in the present Covenant, without distinction of any kind, such as race, colour, sex, language, religion, political or other opinion, national or social origin, property, birth or other status.

---

109 WHO, "Global Report on Ageism" (Geneva, 18 March 2021), 3, https://www.who.int/teams/social-determinants-of-health/demographic-change%20and-healthy-ageing/combatting-ageism/global-report-on-ageism.

110 Barbara Mikołajczyk, "International Human Rights Law and the Intangible Face of Ageism", *Equality, Diversity and Inclusion: An International Journal* 42, No. 3 (28 March 2023): 435, https://doi.org/10.1108/EDI-09-2021-0220.

2. Where not already provided for by existing legislative or other measures, each State Party to the present Covenant undertakes to take the necessary steps, in accordance with its constitutional processes and with the provisions of the present Covenant, to adopt such laws or other measures as may be necessary to give effect to the rights recognized in the present Covenant.
3. Each State Party to the present Covenant undertakes:
   (a) To ensure that any person whose rights or freedoms as herein recognized are violated shall have an effective remedy, notwithstanding that the violation has been committed by persons acting in an official capacity;
   (b) To ensure that any person claiming such a remedy shall have his right thereto determined by competent judicial, administrative or legislative authorities, or by any other competent authority provided for by the legal system of the State, and to develop the possibilities of judicial remedy;
   (c) To ensure that the competent authorities shall enforce such remedies when granted."

Interpreting the states' obligations arising from Article 2, the Human Rights Committee, in its General Comment No. 31 on the nature of the general legal obligation imposed on states parties to the covenant, stressed that the parties should protect individuals, not only against violations of the covenant rights by its agents but also against acts committed by private individuals or entities. In addition, a state fails to ensure the rights by permitting or not taking appropriate measures or exercising due diligence to prevent, punish, investigate or redress the harm caused by such acts by individuals or entities. The committee also stressed that the requirement under Article 2, paragraph 2 to take steps to achieve the covenant rights is unqualified and of immediate effect. Non-compliance with these obligations cannot be justified by reference to political, social, cultural or economic circumstances within the state. It means that a state party must respect, protect and fulfil the rights stipulated in the covenant.[111]

Another provision of principal importance is Article 26 of the ICCPR "All persons are equal before the law and are entitled without any discrimination to the equal protection of the law. In this respect, the law shall

111 Human Rights Committee, "General Comment No. 31. The Nature of the General Legal Obligation Imposed on States Parties to the Covenant Adopted on 29 March 2004 (2187th Meeting), CCPR/C/21/Rev.1/Add. 13", https://digitallibrary.un.org/record/533996.

prohibit any discrimination and guarantee to all persons equal and effective protection against discrimination on any ground such as race, colour, sex, language, religion, political or other opinion, national or social origin, property, birth or other status."

Like Article 2, it indicates "race" and "national origin", but it does not itemise "age" as a premise for non-discrimination. Therefore, only the premise of "other status" could be taken into account as the grounds for a prohibition on age discrimination. However, for years, covering the age premise by "other status" encountered a great deal of resistance from states and international bodies to breaking through into international jurisprudence and the interpretation of international human treaty bodies,[112] including the Human Rights Committee (HCR) and the Committee on Economic, Social and Cultural Rights (CESCR).[113]

It should be also noted that, according to Article 26, the non-discrimination clause is not limited to the rights contained in the covenant, but prohibits discrimination as such, also in the social sphere.[114] The overview of the Human Rights Committee's output shows that the committee considered cases referring to such rights as the rights to work, social security, housing, health, and education.[115] Moreover, the Human Rights Committee, in its General Comment No. 18 pointed out as follows "...the principle of equality sometimes requires States Parties to take affirmative action in order to diminish or eliminate conditions which cause or help to perpetuate discrimination prohibited by the Covenant.

112 Barbara Mikołajczyk, "International Law and Ageism", *Polish Yearbook of International Law* 35 (2015): 83–107, https://doi.org/doi.org/10.7420/pyil2015c.

113 CESCR, "General Comment No. 20: Non-Discrimination in Economic, Social and Cultural Rights (Art. 2, Para. 2), of the International Covenant on Economic, Social and Cultural Rights, E/C.12/GC/20", 2009, 20, https://www.refworld.org/docid/4a60961f2.html.

114 Paul O'Connell, *Vindicating Socio-Economic Rights: International Standards and Comparative Experiences*, Routledge Research in Human Rights Law (Milton Park, Abingdon, Oxon ; New York: Routledge, 2012), 45.

115 Martin Scheinin, "Human Rights Committee Not Only a Committee on Civil and Political Rights," in *Social Rights Jurisprudence: Emerging Trends in International and Comparative Law*, ed. Malcolm Langford (Cambridge; New York: Cambridge University Press, 2008), 540–52.

For example, in a State where the general conditions of a certain part of the population prevent or impair their enjoyment of human rights, the State should take specific action to correct those conditions. Such action may involve granting for a time to the part of the population concerned certain preferential treatment in specific matters as compared with the rest of the population."[116]

Meanwhile, Article 2 of the International Covenant on Economic, Social and Cultural Rights is the central provision that formulates the states' obligations towards economic, social and cultural rights stipulated in the covenant and helps to understand the nature of the whole economic, social and cultural rights as such. It stipulates as follows:

1. Each State Party to the present Covenant undertakes to take steps, individually and through international assistance and co-operation, especially economic and technical, to the maximum of its available resources, with a view to achieving progressively the full realization of the rights recognised in the present Covenant by all appropriate means, including particularly the adoption of legislative measures.
2. The States Parties to the present Covenant undertake to guarantee that the rights enunciated in the present Covenant will be exercised without discrimination of any kind as to race, colour, sex, language, religion, political or other opinion, national or social origin, property, birth or other status.
3. Developing countries, with due regard to human rights and their national economy, may determine to what extent they would guarantee the economic rights recognised in the present Covenant to non-nationals.

Thus, states should act in order to achieve the rights stipulated in the covenant in full, regardless, among other things, of a person's race, colour, language, national or social origin, birth or other status. As in the ICCPR, "age" is not indicated. Therefore, the interpretation of "other status", as provided by the CESCR, is principal for people who experience discrimination due to their age in combination with their migration status. In the General Comment No. 20, the committee defines multiple discrimination (para. 17), refers to age and old age (para. 29) and, finally,

116 Human Rights Committee, para. 10.

recognises "other status" (para. 27) as "intersectional discrimination."[117] It explains:

> "The nature of discrimination varies according to context and evolves over time. A flexible approach to the ground of "other status" is thus needed in order to capture other forms of differential treatment that cannot be reasonably and objectively justified and are of a comparable nature to the expressly recognized grounds in article 2, paragraph 2. These additional grounds are commonly recognized when they reflect the experience of social groups that are vulnerable and have suffered and continue to suffer marginalization. The Committee's general comments and concluding observations have recognized various other grounds and these are described in more detail below. However, this list is not intended to be exhaustive. Other possible prohibited grounds could include the denial of a person's legal capacity because he or she is in prison, or is involuntarily interned in a psychiatric institution, or the intersection of two prohibited grounds of discrimination, e.g. where access to a social service is denied on the basis of sex and disability."[118]

As the list of grounds for discrimination is open, there is also a space for combating discrimination against older migrants in the enjoyment of their social rights.

Traditionally, these rights are perceived as being programmatic by nature and dependent on positive state action and resources. The nature of the obligations arising from the covenant is interpreted by the Committee on Economic, Social and Cultural Rights (CESCR) in its concluding observations addressed to particular states, as well as in the general comments, and mainly in General Comment No. 3 and General Comment No. 24.[119] These obligations are different from those contained in Article 2 of the ICCPR, which requires an immediate obligation to respect and ensure all relevant rights. According to Article 2 of the IESCR, the full realisation of the relevant rights may be achieved progressively, but steps towards

117 CESCR, "General Comment No. 20: Non-Discrimination in Economic, Social and Cultural Rights (Art. 2, Para. 2), of the International Covenant on Economic, Social and Cultural Rights, E/C.12/GC/20".

118 CESCR, para. 27.

119 CESCR, "General Comment No. 24 on State Obligations under the International Covenant on Economic, Social and Cultural Rights in the Context of Business Activities, E/C.12/GC/24", 2017, para 11, https://tbinternet.ohchr.org/_layouts/15/treatybodyexternal/Download.aspx?symbolno=INT%2fCESCR%2fGEC%2f4758&Lang=en.

that goal must be taken within a reasonably short time, and they should be deliberate, specific and targeted as clearly as possible towards meeting the obligations recognised in the covenant. At the same time, a state cannot use the concept of "progressive realisation" as a pretext for non-compliance.[120]

The CESCR paid a good deal of attention to the concept of the "minimum core obligations." The committee applies the minimum core standard when evaluating state compliance under the state-reporting process, in its views issued in individual cases and in the general comments.[121] This explanation of the minimum core obligations is of principal importance as older migrants are often the poorest in the hosting society. The UN Secretary-General noted in one of his reports "…the single most pressing human rights challenge for older persons is poverty. Homelessness, malnutrition, unattended chronic diseases, lack of access to safe drinking water and san itation, unaffordable medicines and treatment, and income insecurity are just a few of the most critical human rights issues that a large number of older persons confront on a daily basis."[122]

Thus, the primary duty of a state is to take steps to achieve the minimum core of obligations, and only later the other (peripherical) elements of rights. A state must demonstrate that every effort has been made to use all the resources at its disposal to satisfy these minimum obligations as a matter of priority. In its General Comment No. 3, the CESCR provided an example of failing to discharge obligations under the covenant. It may happen when any significant number of individuals are deprived of essential foodstuffs, essential primary healthcare, basic shelter and housing, or the

120 CESCR, "Committee on Economic Social and Cultural Rights. General Comment No. 3: The Nature of States Parties' Obligations (Art. 2, Para. 1, of the Covenant)", 1990, para. 2 https://tbinternet.ohchr.org/_layouts/15/treatybodyexternal/Download.aspx?symbolno=INT%2fCESCR%2fGEC%2f4758&Lang=en.

121 Joie Chowdhury, "Unpacking the Minimum Core and Reasonableness Standards", in *Research Handbook on International Law and Social Rights*, Christina Binder, Jane A. Hofbauer, Flávia Piovesan, Amaya Úbeda de Torres (Cheltenham, UK ; Northampton, Massachusetts, USA: Edward Elgar Publishing Limited, 2020), 251–74.

122 UN Secretary General, "Follow-up to the Second World Assembly on Ageing Report of the Secretary-General, 22 July 2011, A/66/173, para. 9."

most basic forms of education.[123] Certainly, internally or internationally displaced children and older persons are the most vulnerable, especially if they leave their place of residence or home country as part of gross migration movements, due to wars, gross human rights violations and natural catastrophes. In such extreme circumstances, the protection of human dignity should be a guiding principle for host states and other stakeholders. In such extreme circumstances, the protection of human dignity should be a guiding principle for host states and other stakeholders. However, for this to happen, they need to be recognised by decision-makers and their voices heard. In this context, an excellent summary is the opinion of Asbjørn Eide, who stressed that "efforts to ensure the enjoyment of economic and social rights for the vulnerable must respect their dignity, focusing on helping them to identify and implement their own solutions to their problems. Their potential energy and resourcefulness, in situations where they can enjoy the basic necessities of adequate food, shelter and education, can be put to more productive use, rather than recourse to hand-outs, which add to their self-depreciation."[124]

Various measures that states should take to make the economic, social, and cultural rights real were indicated by the CESCR in 1995 in its general comments No. 6, which were devoted exclusively to the rights of older persons. The committee described the scope of states' obligations under the covenant and indicated the areas crucial for older persons. However, it does not refer to older migrants or older persons in emergencies.[125]

The best solution in order to make older migrants visible on the international forum is adopting a treaty on older persons' rights, which would also indicate older people's rights in migratory situations, particularly in forced migration. The increased visibility of older persons on the universal forum

---

123 CESCR, "General Comment No. 3: The Nature of States Parties' Obligations (Art. 2, Para. 1, of the Covenant)," para. 10.

124 Asbjørn Eide, "Economic and Social Rights", in *Human Rights: Concepts and Standards*, Symonides, Janusz (Dartmouth: UNESCO Publishing/ Ashgate, 2000), 160–61.

125 CESCR, "Committee on Economic Social and Cultural Rights, General Comment No. 6: The Economic, Social and Cultural Rights of Older Persons, E/1996/22", 8 December 1995, https://www.refworld.org/docid/4538838f11.html.

appears to be the first step to counteracting ageism and discrimination against older persons in various situations, including migration. However, as noted above, there is no universal treaty on the protection of the rights of older persons, either in times of war or peace. Therefore, the model of non-discrimination provisions adopted in other treaties protecting other categories of vulnerable persons may serve as a guide.

The triad of obligations, "respect", "protect" and "fulfil", mentioned at the beginning of this section, is articulated, among other places, in the Convention on the Elimination of All Forms of Discrimination against Women of 1979 (CEDAW),[126] and the Convention on the Rights of Persons with Disabilities (CRPD),[127] and explained by the human rights treaty bodies in their general comments and recommendations. For example, the CRPD stipulates "that the effective enjoyment of the rights to equality and non-discrimination calls for the adoption of enforcement measures" and indicates a long list of steps that should be taken by states in this area.[128]

Meanwhile, the CEDAW Committee explains that "states parties to the Convention are under a legal obligation to respect, protect, promote and fulfil this right to non-discrimination for women and to ensure the development and advancement of women in order to improve their position to one of de jure as well as de facto equality with men."[129]. Moreover, it also notes that "states parties have an obligation not to cause discrimination

126 United Nations, Convention on the Elimination of All Forms of Discrimination against Women, New York, 18 December 1979, UNTS, vol. 1249, p. 13, https://treaties.un.org/Pages/ViewDetails.aspx?src=TREATY&mtdsg_no=IV-8&chapter=4&clang=_en.

127 United Nations, "Convention on the Rights of Persons with Disabilities, New York, 13 December 2006, UNTS, 2515, vol. 2515, p. 3, https://www.ohchr.org/EN/HRBodies/CRPD/Pages/ConventionRightsPersonsWithDisabilities.aspx.

128 CRPD, "Committee on the Rights of Persons with Disabilities, General Comment No. 6 (2018) on Equality and Non-Discrimination, CRPD/C/GC/6", 2018, para. 31, https://tbinternet.ohchr.org/_layouts/15/TreatyBodyExternal/TBSearch.aspx?Lang=en&TreatyID=4&DocTypeCategoryID=7.

129 CEDAW Committee, "General Recommendation No. 25 on Article 4, Paragraph 1, of the Convention (Temporary Special Measures) Core, CEDAW/C/GC/28", 2004, para. 4, https://tbinternet.ohchr.org/_layouts/15/treatybodyexternal/TBSearch.aspx?Lang=en&TreatyID=3&DocTypeID=11.

against women through acts or omissions; they are further obliged to react actively against discrimination against women, regardless of whether such acts or omissions are perpetrated by the State or by private actors"[130]

The CEDAW Committee stressed the multiple forms of discrimination against women in its General Recommendation No. 27 of 2010, dedicated exclusively to older women. The committee outlined the content of the states' obligations concerning ageing with dignity and older women's rights. It formulated the policy recommendations aimed at mainstreaming the responses to the concerns of older women into national strategies, development initiatives and positive action so that older women can fully participate in society without discrimination and on an equal basis with men. It explained that "states parties should adopt appropriate gender- and age-sensitive laws and policies to ensure the protection of older women with refugee status or who are stateless, as well as those who are internally displaced or are migrant workers."[131]

The International Convention on the Protection of the Rights of All Migrant Workers and Members of Their Families of 1990, mentioned in the introduction above, also obliges states not only to "respect" the migrants' rights but also to "ensure" them. Article 7 of this convention is crucial here as it stipulates that "States Parties undertake, in accordance with the international instruments concerning human rights, to respect and to ensure to all migrant workers and members of their families within their territory or subject to their jurisdiction the rights provided for in the present Convention without distinction of any kind such as to sex, race, colour, language, religion or conviction, political or other opinion, national, ethnic or social origin, nationality, age, economic position, property, marital status, birth or other status."

130 CEDAW Committee, "General Recommendation No. 28 on the Core Obligations of States Parties under Article 2 of the Convention on the Elimination of All Forms of Discrimination against Women, CEDAW/C/GC/28", 2010, https://undocs.org/CEDAW/C/GC/28.

131 CEDAW Committee, "General Recommendation No 27 on Older Women and Protection of Their Human Rights, CEDAW/C/GC/27", 2010, para. 50, https://documents-dds-ny.un.org/doc/UNDOC/GEN/G10/472/53/PDF/G1047253.pdf?OpenElement.

Worth noting is that the convention indicates "age" as a premise of non-discrimination, which is unique in the currently binding human rights treaties. However, the Committee on the Protection of the Rights of All Migrant Workers and Members of their Families (CMW), when interpreting the convention, failed to explain the scope of states' obligations in the area of non-discrimination of migrant workers, nor referred to older workers' rights. The committee does invoke General Comment No. 15 of the Human Rights Committee entitled "The position of aliens under the Covenant" of 1986, in which the Human Rights Committee makes clear that there must be no discrimination between aliens and citizens in the application of the human rights contained in the ICCPR.[132] The CMW also refers to General Recommendation No. 30 of the Committee on the Elimination of Racial Discrimination ("Discrimination against non-citizens") of 2004, in which it makes specific recommendations to state parties to eliminate discrimination against non-citizens.[133]

In migration matters, where migrants are often people of other nationalities, ethnicities, colours and races, the scope of states' responsibilities is highly complex. Prohibiting racial discrimination does not imply equal rights for citizens and for migrants without citizenship. On the other hand, the prohibition on racial discrimination has particular power as a peremptory norm of general international law,[134] as well as a customary norm establishing obligations *erga omnes*, i.e. owed to the international

---

132 Human Rights Committee, "General Comment CCPR, General Comment No. 15: The Position of Aliens Under the Covenant, 11 April 1986", https://www.refworld.org/docid/45139acfc.html.

133 The Committee on the Elimination of Racial Discrimination, "General Recommendation 30, Discrimination against Non-Citizens, 64th Session, 23 February-12 March 2004, CERD/C/64/Misc.11/Rev.3", 2004, https://www.google.com/url?sa=t&rct=j&q=&esrc=s&source=web&cd=&ved=2ahUKEwip2vf55dODAxWwKBAIHQ-cDb8QFnoECBEQAQ&url=https%3A%2F%2Fwww2.ohchr.org%2Fenglish%2Fbodies%2Fcerd%2Fdocs%2Fcerd-gc30.doc&usg=AOvVaw3yedj6egtj76SvAuyFH-ic&opi=89978449.

134 International and Law Commission, "Report of the International Law Commission Seventy-First Session (29 April–7 June and 8 July–9 August 2019)", 2019, 147.

community as a whole.[135] In addition, the prohibition on racial discrimination cannot be derogated by government actions (e.g. immigration policies), national laws or even international agreements. Thus, the peremptory character of the prohibition on racial discrimination affects (or should affect) the interpretation of states' obligations in the area of migration under human rights treaties.

Certainly, the prohibition on racial discrimination is a core issue of the International Convention on the Elimination of All Forms of Racial Discrimination of 1965 (CERD),[136] though it does not mention migrants, aliens or non-nationals. What is more, according to Article 1 sec. 2 and 3, the CERD "does not apply to distinctions, exclusions, restrictions or preferences made by a State Party to this Convention between citizens and non-citizens. Nothing in this Convention may be interpreted as affecting in any way the legal provisions of States Parties concerning nationality, citizenship or naturalization, provided that such provisions do not discriminate against any particular nationality."

Thus, the CERD committee confirms that aliens, including migrants, may be treated differently than nationals, but on an equal basis, without giving preference to any group on racial or ethnic grounds. Given the convention's objectives and purposes, the criteria for any differentiation should have a legitimate aim and be proportional to achieving this aim.[137]

---

135 Steven Wheatley, *The Idea of International Human Rights Law*, 1st ed. (Oxford University Press, 2019), 129, https://doi.org/10.1093/oso/9780198749844.001.0001.

136 United Nations, "Convention on the Elimination of All Forms of Discrimination a Racial Discrimination (adopted by the UNGA resolution 2106 (XX) 21 December 1965), New York, 7 March December 1966, UNTS vol. 660, p. 195," https://www.refworld.org/docid/3ae6b3940.html.

137 The Committee on the Elimination of Racial Discrimination, "General Recommendation 30, Discrimination against Non-Citizens, 64th Session, 23 February-12 March 2004, para. 4, CERD/C/64/Misc.11/Rev.3", https://www.google.com/url?sa=t&rct=j&q=&esrc=s&source=web&cd=&ved=2ahUKEwip2vf55dODAxWwKBAIHQ-cDb8QFnoECBEQAQ&url=https%3A%2F%2Fwww2.ohchr.org%2Fenglish%2Fbodies%2Fcerd%2Fdocs%2Fcerd-gc30.doc&usg=AOvVaw3yedj6egtj76SvAuyFH-ic&opi=89978449.

These problematic relationships between the prohibition on racial discrimination and migrants' status have been highlighted, among others, by Colm O'Cinneide[138] and by David Fennelly and Clíodhna Murphy,[139] especially concerning irregular migration, which causes unresolved tensions. They indicate the above-mentioned General Recommendation No. 30 of the Committee on the Elimination of Racial Discrimination, which opened up new legal and political avenues for the protection of migrants' rights, although the convention does not mention migrants.[140] In the recommendation, the committee invokes the Durban Declaration, in which the World Conference against Racism, Racial Discrimination, Xenophobia and Related Intolerance recognised that xenophobia against non-nationals, particularly migrants, refugees and asylum seekers, constitutes one of the main sources of contemporary racism and human rights violations.[141]

In addition, when explaining the meaning of non-discrimination concerning non-nationals, the committee explained that states should understand that in certain circumstances, discrimination may consist of a denial

---

138 Colm O'Cinneide, "The Human Rights of Migrants with Irregular Status: Giving Substance to Aspirations of Universalism", in *Migrants with Irregular Status in Europe*, ed. Sarah Spencer and Anna Triandafyllidou, IMISCOE Research Series (Cham: Springer International Publishing, 2020), 55, https://doi.org/10.1007/978-3-030-34324-8_4.

139 David Fennelly and Clíodhna Murphy, "Racial Discrimination and Nationality and Migration Exceptions: Reconciling CERD and the Race Equality Directive", *Netherlands Quarterly of Human Rights* 39, No. 4 (December 2021): 308–28, https://doi.org/10.1177/09240519211055648.

140 Fennelly and Murphy, 317; O'Cinneide, "The Human Rights of Migrants with Irregular Status", 63.

141 In the Durban Declaration, states were called upon "To take all possible measures to promote the full enjoyment by all migrants of all human rights, including those related to fair wages and equal remuneration for work of equal value without distinction of any kind, and to the right to security in the event of unemployment, sickness, disability, widowhood, old age or other lack of livelihood in circumstances beyond their control, social security, including social insurance, access to education, health care, social services and respect for their cultural identity." United Nations, "World Conference Against Racism, Racial Discrimination, Xenophobia and Related Intolerance", 2001, para. 16, https://www.ohchr.org/sites/default/files/Documents/Publications/Durban_text_en.pdf.

of citizenship for long-term or permanent residents resulting, among other things, in creating disadvantages for access to employment and social benefits (para. 17). The committee also indicated that states should remove obstacles that prevent the enjoyment of economic, social and cultural rights by non-citizens, including in the areas of housing and health (paras. 29 and 36).

3.2. European developments

The European Convention for the Protection of Human Rights and Fundamental Freedoms of 1950, like the ICCPR, contains civil and political rights (though the right to education appeared in the first additional protocol to the ECHR). Its antidiscrimination clause (Article 14) sets out "race", "nationality", "national or social origin", "association with national minority", "colour" and "language" as the grounds of non-discrimination that are well embedded in all universal and regional treaties and are usually or often associated with a migratory status. On the other hand, Article 14 fails to indicate "age" as a premise of non-discrimination. It states that "The enjoyment of the rights and freedoms set forth in this Convention shall be secured without discrimination on any ground such as sex, race, colour, language, religion, political or other opinion, national or social origin, association with a national minority, property, birth or other status."

This provision does not have an autonomous character and the ban on discrimination is strictly tied to the rights and freedoms contained in the convention and its protocols.[142] For this reason, it should be noted that the convention does not contain the right to seek asylum or the right to leave

142 The ECHR and its protocols set out the rights to life, freedom and security, respect for private and family life, freedom of expression, freedom of thought, conscience and religion, vote in and stand for election, a fair trial in civil and criminal matters, property and peaceful enjoyment of possessions. In addition to the prohibition on discrimination in the enjoyment of the rights and freedoms secured by the convention, it prohibits the death penalty, torture or inhuman or degrading treatment or punishment, slavery and forced labour, arbitrary and unlawful detention, deportation of a state's own nationals or denying them entry and the collective deportation of foreigners.

a country. However, Additional Protocol No. 12 to the ECHR of 2000[143] goes beyond the scope of the convention and expands the scope of non-discrimination to include situations where: the enjoyment of any right is specifically granted to an individual under national law; there is a clear obligation of a public authority under national law to behave in a particular manner; a public authority exercises its discretionary power; or in the case of other act or omission by a public authority.[144] Undoubtedly, this expansion of the prohibition on discrimination is crucial for individuals in immigration situations of many types, despite the European Court of Human Rights (ECtHR) repeatedly stressing that the convention does not guarantee the right of an alien to enter or settle in a particular country.[145]

The premise of "age" as a new ground for non-discrimination has not been added to the list of non-discrimination grounds in Protocol No. 12. Thus again, "other status" should be employed to protect older persons against age discrimination. As a result, protecting older migrants against discrimination and establishing the scope of states' obligations in this area, requires some interpretative work.

Article 1 of the ECHR makes a very succinct reference to the states' obligations. It stipulates that state parties "shall secure to everyone within their jurisdiction the rights and freedoms defined in Section I of this Convention." In this way, specific legal obligations have been imposed on states. Their fulfilment is ensured by using control mechanisms – the European Court of Human Rights (and previously also the European Commission of Human Rights). It means that the case law here plays a

143 Council of Europe, "Protocol No. 12 to the Convention for the Protection of Human Rights and Fundamental Freedoms, Rome, 4 November 2000", (Council of Europe Treaty Series No. 177),https://www.coe.int/en/web/conventions/full-list?module=signatures-by-treaty&treatynum=177. Only 20 of 46 Council of Europe member states are parties to the protocol (March 2024).

144 Council of Europe, "Explanatory Report to the Protocol No. 12 to the Convention for the Protection of Human Rights and Fundamental Freedoms, Rome, 4 November 2000" (Council of Europe Treaty Series No. 177), para. 22.

145 European Court of Human Rights, "Guide on Article 14 of the European Convention on Human Rights and on Article 1 of Protocol No. 12 to the Convention, 31 August 2022", para. 229, https://www.echr.coe.int/documents/d/echr/Guide_Art_14_Art_1_Protocol_12_ENG.

crucial role in shaping the states' obligations.[146] Thus, despite the lack of reference to older persons or the premise of "age" as a prohibition on discrimination in the ECHR text, this treaty can still be the basis for deriving positive obligations of states concerning older persons, including those "on the move" or those with immigrant origins. Over the years, the ECtHR has worked out interpretative tools to adjust the treaty to new circumstances and supplement its provisions with new understanding. This is possible due to the doctrine of the "living instrument", "dynamic" and "evolutive" interpretation of the convention and, finally, the doctrine of the "margin of appreciation." These concepts have often provoked dissatisfaction among states due to uncertainty about their obligations and raising the ongoing debate about the proper limits of the court's interpretative jurisdiction among academics, and even among the ECtHR's judges.[147] On the other hand, they have the potential to help judges establish the states' obligations toward older migrants, taking into account their specific situation and vulnerabilities.

However, a quantitative and descriptive analysis of cases considered by the ECtHR in the first decade of the 21st century shows that about 12 % of all the ECtHR's judgements referred to older persons and the court ruled that there had been a violation of human rights in a significant majority of them.[148] At the same time, the ECtHR considered many complaints submitted by immigrants or asylum seekers,[149] despite the fact that, like the covenants, the ECHR does not set out the right to asylum and does not

---

146 Andrew Z. Drzemczewski, *European Human Rights Convention in Domestic Law: A Comparative Study* (Oxford University Press, 1983), 22; Vesna Stefanovska, "Retrospective of the Dynamic and Evolutive Interpretation of ECHR: Framing the Strasbourg's Interpretative Ethic", *Iustinianus Primus Law Review* 11, No. 1 (2020): 4.

147 Mikołajczyk, *Social Inclusion for Older Persons and Human Rights Law. The Potential for Universal and European Instruments*, 99.

148 Benny Spanier, Israel Doron, and Faina Milman-Sivan, "Older Persons' Use of the European Court of Human Rights", *Journal of Cross Cultural Gerontology* 28 (2013): 416, https://doi.org/10.1007/s10823-013-9212-7.

149 David Moya and Georgios Milios, eds., "Social Rights and Migrants before the European Court of Human Rights", in *Aliens before the European Court of Human Rights* (Brill | Nijhoff, 2021), 191–210, https://doi.org/10.1163/9789004465695_010.

set out the right to leave a country, including one's own country. On the other hand, older migrants are usually not the authors of complaints, or at least the combination of their age and their migratory situation does not constitute a central issue of the case.[150]

Cases involving older people, where their age is an important circumstance, are sometimes found in connection with Article 3 (prohibition on torture and degrading treatment) and with Article 8 (respect for family life) in the context of deportation and family reunification. Generally, the ECtHR accepts the differences determined by migration categories at the national level, but protects more vulnerable people when the sponsor or applicant has received international protection or been an asylum seeker.[151] Of course, the court's decision depends on the circumstances of the case. For example, in *Chvzhevska v. Sweden*, the applicant, a 91-year-old Ukrainian national, made an allegation that the execution of a deportation order to Ukraine would constitute a violation of Articles 3 and 8 of the convention due to her poor health and lack of relatives and other acquaintances in Ukraine.[152] In the case of *Frolova v. Finland*, the applicant, a Russian national born in 1935, argued that she was entirely dependent on her family in Finland and that her deportation to Russia would have serious consequences.[153] In both cases, the ECtHR decided to strike out the complaints from the list, as the cases found a domestic solution, with both applicants being granted residence permits. The ECtHR ruled on the merits, among other things, in the case of *Senchishak v. Finland*, concerning the threatened expulsion from Finland of a 72-year-old Russian national. The court did not share

150 Council of Europe/European Court of Human Rights, "Guide on the Case-Law of the European Convention on Human Rights. Immigration. 31 August 2022", https://www.echr.coe.int/documents/d/echr/Guide_Immigration_ENG.

151 Jaana Palander, "Recognizing Insecurities of Family Members Abroad: Human Rights Balancing in European and Finnish Case Law", in *Forced Migration and Separated Families*, ed. Marja Tiilikainen et al., IMISCOE Research Series (Cham: Springer International Publishing, 2023), 43, https://doi.org/10.1007/978-3-031-24974-7_3.

152 European Court of Human Rights, "*Ganna Petrovna Chvzhevska v. Sweden*, Application No. 60794/11, Decision, 25 September 2012".

153 European Court of Human Rights, "*Rimma Frolova v. Finland*, Application No. 47772/11, Decision, 14 January 2014".

the applicant's arguments on the lack of access to medical care in Russia, the inability to obtain a place in a nursing home and the separation from her daughter, a Finnish citizen. The court found that there would be no violation of Article 3 of the Convention if the applicant was deported to Russia and argued that neither the general situation in Russia nor the applicant's circumstances would expose her to the threat of inhumane or degrading treatment if she were expelled. In particular, the applicant had not provided evidence supporting her allegations that she would not have access to medical care in Russia.[154]

Another example of where older age combined with migration in the context of non-discrimination is the case of *Pichkur v. Ukraine*. The applicant, having worked for forty years in Ukraine, retired and began receiving a retirement pension. As a pensioner, he emigrated to Germany. He complained that his pension payments were terminated on the grounds that he had been permanently resident abroad. The ECtHR stated that the rise of population mobility, higher levels of international cooperation and integration, as well as developments in the area of banking services and information technologies no longer justify largely technically motivated restrictions in respect of beneficiaries of social security payments living abroad.[155]

This case shows that, although the convention does contain social rights, including the right to social security, the ECtHR may consider "social cases". This should be recognised as proof of the indivisibility of human rights. On the other hand, the court confirms the wide margin of appreciation accorded to states in the area of social rights when choosing the measures necessary to effectively implement rights and freedoms.[156]

---

154 European Court of Human Rights, "*Senchishak v. Finland*, Application No. 5049/12, Judgement, 18 November 2014 (Final 23 March 2015)", 2014.

155 European Court of Human Rights, "*Pichkur v. Ukraine,* Application No. 10441/06, Judgement 7 November 2013, (Final 07 February 2014)", para. 53, http://hudoc.echr.coe.int/eng#{%22itemid%22:[%22001-127810 %22]}.

156 See more: Ingrid Leijten, *Core Socio-Economic Rights and the European Court of Human Rights. In Core Socio-Economic Rights and the European Court of Human Rights*, Cambridge Studies in European Law and Policy (Cambridge: Cambridge University Press, 2018); Ellie Palmer, "Protecting Socio-Economic Rights Through the European Convention on Human Rights: Trends and Developments in the European Court of Human Rights",

On the European forum, the European Social Charter of 1961[157] and the (Revised) European Social Charter of 1996[158] are the main treaties that safeguard socio-economic rights of crucial importance for older migrants. The Revised Charter introduced an antidiscrimination clause (Article E) to the European social law framework. It proclaims that "The enjoyment of the rights set forth in this Charter shall be secured without discrimination on any ground such as race, colour, sex, language, religion, political or other opinion, national extraction or social origin, health, association with a national minority, birth or other status."

Article E prohibits not only direct discrimination, but also all forms of indirect discrimination. As with Article 14 of the ECHR, the purpose of Article E is to ensure the equal and effective enjoyment of all the rights it applies to, irrespective of the particular characteristics of specific individuals or groups of individuals. As in the case of the ECHR, the list of these characteristics is not exhaustive, as shown by the presence of "other status." The European Committee of Social Rights, which monitors and controls compliance with the charter, has included, for example, asexuality, pregnancy and ethnicity in this rationale. In addition, the committee took an expansive approach to grounds of intersectional discrimination. Of particular relevance to older migrants of various types is the committee's position that states parties violate the charter when, without objective and reasonable justification, they fail to treat differently persons whose situations differ significantly, and that human differences in a democratic society should

Erasmus Law Review 2, No. 4 (2009): 397–425, https://papers.ssrn.com/sol3/papers.cfm?abstract_id=1542674; Elena Sychenko, "Enlarging the Scope of the European Convention on Human Rights: History, Philosophical Roots and Practical Outcomes", *Zbornik Pravnog Fakulteta u Zagrebu* 65, No. 2 (2015): 309–26, https://www.scopus.com/record/display.uri?eid=2-s2.0-84938949059&origin=inward&txGid=720db1608d11cd12d443900599582c43.

157 Council of Europe, "European Social Charter, Turin 18 October 1961" (European Treaty Series – No. 035), https://www.coe.int/en/web/conventions/full-list?module=treaty-detail&treatynum=035.

158 Council of Europe, "European Social Charter (Revised)v Strasbourg, 03 May 1996" (Council of Europe Treaty Series – No. 163).

not only be viewed positively, but should be treated with discernment to ensure real and effective equality.[159]

Finally, both social charters contain Article 19 protecting the rights of migrant workers who are nationals of a state party and their families to protection and assistance in the territory of any other party. The personal scope of this provision is limited to nationals of a Council of Europe member state (a party to the charters), who lawfully reside or work regularly within the territory of other Council of Europe member states, also bound by this treaty. Thus, migrant workers from other states are not covered by this treaty. However, in 2004 the committee set out the possibility of extending the protection of the charters to aliens from states not parties to the charter by guaranteeing them rights identical to or inseparable from those contained in the charter through the ratification of human rights treaties, in particular the European Convention on Human Rights, or through the adoption of national, constitutional, legislative or other legislation. The committee clarified that, in certain specific situations, the implementation of certain provisions may require complete equality of treatment between nationals and aliens, in particular refugees within the meaning of the 1951 Geneva Convention relating to the Status of Refugees and lawfully resident therein and stateless persons, as defined in the 1954 New York Convention relating to the Status of Stateless Persons.[160]

The committee also explained that the limitation on the personal scope should not be interpreted in such a way as to deprive aliens belonging to the category of irregular migrants of the protection of the most fundamental rights enshrined in the Charter, or impair their fundamental rights such as the right to life and physical integrity, or the right to human dignity. The limitation of the personal scope should be interpreted in good faith and in harmony with other relevant and applicable principles of international law, including, first and foremost, the peremptory norms of general international

159 Council of Europe, *Digest of the Case Law of the European Committee of Social Rights*, 2022, 210.

160 United Nations, "Convention Relating to the Status of Stateless Persons New York, 28 September 1954, UNTS vol. 360, p. 117", https://treaties.un.org/Pages/ViewDetailsII.aspx?src=TREATY&mtdsg_no=V-3&chapter=5&Temp=mtdsg2&clang=_en.

law, which take precedence over all other international norms and from which no derogation is permitted.[161] This, therefore, implies compliance with the prohibition of racial discrimination cited above.

Contrary to the universal and the European regional international treaty law, the EU law contains "age" as a premise for non-discrimination. It has been introduced into the EU primary law, the Treaty on European Union, the Treaty on the Functioning of the European Union – TFEU[162] and the Charter of Fundamental Rights in the European Union – CFREU. A ban on age discrimination was also introduced to secondary EU law – the Council's Directive 2000/78/EC, known as the Equality Employment Directive.[163] This directive sets out a general framework for combating discrimination based on religion or belief, disability, sexual orientation and age. However, it does not go beyond employment and what is more, under certain conditions, it allows for differences in treatment on the grounds of age. According to Age Platform Europe, the EU Member States use this possibility to apply a wide range of exceptions in their legislation discriminating against older workers or candidates for work, meaning that this part of the population is still left behind.[164] This directive should be taken into account when analysing the situation of older migrants, as they are

---

161 Council of Europe, *Digest of the Case Law of the European Committee of Social Rights*, 211.

162 European Union, "Consolidated Versions of the Treaty on European Union and the Treaty on the Functioning of the European Union Consolidated Version of the Treaty on European Union Consolidated Version of the Treaty on the Functioning of the European Union Protocols Annexes to the Treaty on the Functioning of the European Union Declarations Annexed to the Final Act of the Intergovernmental Conference Which Adopted the Treaty of Lisbon, Signed on 13 December 2007 Tables of Equivalences, O. J. of the European Union (2016/C 202/01)" (European Union, 2007), https://eur-lex.europa.eu/legal-content/EN/TXT/?uri=celex%3A12016ME%2FTXT.

163 European Union, "Council Directive 2000/78/EC of 27 November 2000 Establishing a General Framework for Equal Treatment in Employment and Occupation O. J. L 303, 02.12.2000, p. 16 – 22", https://eur-lex.europa.eu/legal-content/EN/TXT/?uri=celex%3A32000L0078.

164 Age Platform Europe, "The Right to Work in Old Age: How the EU Employment Framework Directive Still Leaves Older Workers behind, March 2021", 2021, https://www.age-platform.eu/barometer-2023/end-age-discrimination-in-employment/.

more likely to work after pension age, often in insecure jobs despite their skills and experience.[165]

The Charter of Fundamental Rights in the European Union not only prohibits age discrimination but, what is unique in the acts not dedicated exclusively to older persons, its Article 25 stipulates that "the Union recognises and respects the rights of the elderly to lead a life of dignity and independence and to participate in social and cultural life."

This provision, part of primary EU law, is essential for older persons. However, compared to other provisions of the CFREU, e.g. those on gender equality and children's rights, it is declaratory and ambiguous in nature. "Recognition" and "respect" may be interpreted differently and do not indicate specific measures towards older persons.

Finally, taking into account the retirement migration of older Europeans within the EU, the EEA and the EFTA area, the principle of non-discrimination on the grounds of nationality, as set out in Article 18 TFEU and Article 21(2) of the Charter of Fundamental Rights should be mentioned. Article 24 of Directive 2004/38/EC gives specific expression to this principle stating that "all Union citizens residing on the basis of this Directive in the territory of the host Member State shall enjoy equal treatment with the nationals of that Member State within the scope of the Treaty. The benefit of this right shall be extended to family members who are not nationals of a Member State and who have the right of residence or permanent residence."[166]

---

165 Age Platform Europe, "Support for Older People in the Labour Market", 2023, https://www.age-platform.eu/barometer-2023/end-age-discrimination-in-employment/.

166 European Union, "Directive 2004/38/EC of the European Parliament and of the Council of 29 April 2004 on the Right of Citizens of the Union and Their Family Members to Move and Reside Freely within the Territory of the Member States Amending Regulation (EEC) No. 1612/68 and Repealing Directives 64/221/EEC, 68/360/EEC, 72/194/EEC, 73/148/EEC, 75/34/EEC, 75/35/EEC, 90/364/EEC, 90/365/EEC and 93/96/EEC" (O. J. L 158, 30.4.2004, pp. 77–113), https://eur-lex.europa.eu/legal-content/PL/TXT/?uri=celex%3A32004L0038.

Certainly, if EU citizens want to reside in another EU Member State (or the EEA and EFTA states), they must meet several conditions.[167] However, in the context of non-discrimination, it may be observed that, while nationality cannot be a reason for distinction, financial resources can. The *Arnulf Clauder* case considered by the EFTA Court is an example of this.[168]

In both the Council of Europe and the European Union, several legal instruments (e.g. EU's Race Equality Directive[169]) have been adopted and institutions set up to eliminate racial discrimination, including the European Commission against Racism and Intolerance (ECRI). In 2016, the latter issued General Policy Recommendation No. 16 on safeguarding irregularly present migrants from discrimination. It aims to ensure that everyone from this particularly vulnerable group has access to those human rights guaranteed to them by international human rights law, in particular in the areas of education, healthcare, housing, social security and social assistance, labour protection and justice, while under the jurisdiction of a Council of

---

167 Sandra Mantu and Paul Minderhoud, "Exploring the Links between Residence and Social Rights for Economically Inactive EU Citizens", *European Journal of Migration and Law* 21, No. 3 (7 August 2019): 313–37, https://www.researchgate.net/publication/335719432_Exploring_the_Links_between_Residence_and_Social_Rights_for_Economically_Inactive_EU_Citizens; Monika Patrycja Bator-Bryła, "Prohibition of Discrimination on Grounds of Nationality in the Freedom of Movement of Persons within the EU in the Light of Case Law of the Court of Justice of the European Union", *Review of European and Comparative Law* 46, No. 3 (21 August 2021): 189–218, https://doi.org/10.31743/recl.12340.

168 It referred to a German pensioner receiving old-age pensions and supplementary welfare benefits in Liechtenstein, who requested a residence permit for his wife, also a German national. His request was turned down because he lacked sufficient resources for himself and his wife not to be a burden on the Liechtenstein social assistance system – Court of Justice of the European Union, "Judgment of the Court of 26 July 2011 in Case E-4/11 – Arnulf Clauder (Directive 2004/38/EC – Family Reunification – Right of Residence for Family Members of EEA Nationals Holding a Right of Permanent Residence – Condition to Have Sufficient Resources) (OJ C, C/344, 24.11.2011, p. 9.", https://eur-lex.europa.eu/legal-content/EN/TXT/?uri=CELEX:E2011J0004).

169 European Union, "Council Directive 2000/43/EC of 29 June 2000 Implementing the Principle of Equal Treatment between Persons Irrespective of Racial or Ethnic Origin, OJ L 180, 19.7.2000, pp. 22–26." (O. J. L 180, 19.7.2000, pp. 22–26), https://eur-lex.europa.eu/legal-content/EN/TXT/?uri=celex%3A32000L0043.

Europe Member State. The recommendation does not indicate the needs of older migrants, with the only category of migrants explicitly mentioned being children.[170]

Meanwhile, the Race Equality Directive aims to lay down a framework for combating discrimination based on racial or ethnic origin to implement the principle of equal treatment in the Member States. However, it does not itemise any specific vulnerable group. What is more, it limits its scope in Article 3 sec. 2. It explains that "this Directive does not cover difference of treatment based on nationality and is without prejudice to provisions and conditions relating to the entry into and residence of third-country nationals and stateless persons on the territory of Member States, and to any treatment which arises from the legal status of the third-country nationals and stateless persons concerned."

As Finnelly and Murphy noted, there is no clear guidance from the CJEU on the proper scope and limits of Article 3 sec. 2, or the extent to which the Race Directive can offer protection to non-nationals living in the EU. As a result, in this area the EU fails to protect against race discrimination for the most vulnerable groups and may serve to entrench, rather than eliminate, some of the most serious forms of race discrimination.[171]

If, therefore, there is no clear indication about the protection of migrants against racial discrimination, it is all the more difficult to expect to find a clear indication under European law about the protection of older migrants against multiple and intersectional discrimination based on race combined with migration status and age.

3.3. Potential for filling gaps

The above review shows that, in the context of the prohibition on discrimination under international treaties, older migrants fall into a gap in human rights protection. They are doubly underserved. International human rights

170 European Commission against Racism and Intolerance (ECRI), "General Policy Recommendation No. 16 on Safeguarding Irregularly Present Migrants from Discrimination" (Council of Europe, 2016), https://rm.coe.int/ecri-general-policy-recommendation-no-16-on-safeguarding-irregularly-p/16808b5b0b.

171 Fennelly and Murphy, "Racial Discrimination and Nationality and Migration Exceptions", 326.

treaties protecting the rights of all humans do not directly identify "age" as a condition for non-discrimination. Interpretive efforts are therefore needed to place "age" in the premise of "other status." As a result, ageism and age discrimination, which encounter interpretative difficulties, overlap with differentiation based on migration status. After all, international law allows for a distinction between the situation of migrants and citizens. In the case of migrants, such a distinction is permissible even in light of the prohibition on racial discrimination.

Indeed, international law guarantees fundamental rights for older migrants, as for all people, though it is challenging to determine the precise obligations of states in the area of the prohibition on discrimination against older migrants in various areas of life. Non-discrimination against vulnerable groups requires states to take steps to ensure that the members of these groups can exercise their human rights. However, concerning social rights in particular, states enjoy a wide margin of discretion, and meeting the needs of older non-nationals usually falls outside the core obligations of states. It raises the question of whether international law has the means to ensure that older migrants have the opportunity to exercise their human rights.

In this respect, it is worth invoking Elvira Domínguez Redondo's view that "a more general phenomenon in international law, that is, that normative progress is often slower than advances made by the institutional monitoring mechanism."[172]

Universal and European human rights laws have at their disposal various incentive, monitoring, and control mechanisms aimed at the domestication of human rights standards in national laws. These are binding and non-binding; they sometimes oblige states to behave in a certain way and, at other times they merely invite them to do so. Their effectiveness depends on a general awareness about them, their application, the capacity of the relevant bodies, and, above all, the will of states to implement them at the domestic level.[173]

---

172 Elvira Domínguez Redondo, "Rethinking the Legal Foundations of Control in International Human Rights Law – The Case of Special Procedures", *Netherlands Quarterly of Human Rights* 29, No. 3 (September 2011): 288, https://doi.org/10.1177/016934411102900302.

173 Hellen Keller and Geir Ulfstein, "Conclusions", in *UN Human Rights Treaty Bodies. Law and Legitimacy Edited by Helen Keller and Geir Ulfstein*

The jurisprudence of international courts, including the ECtHR, can contribute to establishing states' obligations to protect older migrants from discrimination based on their age, the migratory situation they find themselves in, and, in addition, their race and ethnicity. Regardless of nationality and migratory status, individuals can bring human rights complaints against any of the 46 state parties to the ECHR after using up every possible chance of appeal at the national level. If the ECtHR finds that a state violated the applicant's human rights stipulated in the ECHR, a state must provide justice to the applicant and take steps to prevent such violations in the future. The court's purpose in making a judgement is not only to settle a given case, but also to formulate a legal principle that will affect not only a given state but all state parties to the convention.[174] Thus, the ECtHR has significant potential to exert influence on states' behaviour toward older migrants.

The procedure of individual communications with the human rights treaty bodies – the committees of experts established based on the human rights global core treaties – is a similar mechanism. The committees' views may include recommendations of a general nature, in addition to making recommendations on a specific infringement of a treaty provision. The views are not judgements and are classified as non-binding, but when considering individual cases the committees act as *quasi*–judicial bodies and states bound by a given treaty "have legal obligations to attach great legal weight to the finding of the treaty bodies."[175] Potentially, any one of the nine human rights bodies may come across a case in which the particular

(Cambridge: Cambridge University Press, 2012), 418; Rosanne van Alebeek and Andre Nollkaemper, "The Legal Status of Decisions by Human Rights Treaty Bodies in National Law", in *UN Human Rights Treaty Bodies. Law and Legitimacy Edited by Helen Keller and Geir Ulfstein* (Cambridge: Cambridge University Press, 2012), 356–413.

174 Leszek Garlicki, *Konwencja o Ochronie Praw Człowieka i Podstawowych Wolności. Komentarz, Tom II, [Convention for the Protection of Human Rights and Fundamental Freedoms. Commentary, Volume II], Edited by Leszek Garlicki* (Warsaw: C.H. Beck, 2010), 360–61.

175 Geir Ulfstein, "Individual Complaints", in *UN Human Rights Treaty Bodies. Law and Legitimacy Edited by Helen Keller and Geir Ulfstein* (Cambridge: Cambridge University Press, 2012), 115.

situation of an older migrant suffering intersectional discrimination due to the circumstances of age and migratory status is invoked.

Another instrument that has been created under the auspices of the is the system of collective complaints, introduced by the Additional Protocol to the European Social Charter of 1995[176] and overtaken by the Revised European Social Charter. The right to bring a complaint before the European Committee of Social Rights (ECSR) is not granted to individuals, but may be submitted, among others, by representative national non-governmental organisations authorised to pursue statutory activities within a Council of Europe member state. Compared with individual complaints/communications, the collective complaints procedure is simpler and more flexible, for example, exhausting the national legal protection system is not a condition of admissibility. Most importantly, taking into account the gaps in the protection of older migrants and the circumstances of their vulnerabilities, it is crucial that a complaint does not have to refer to a legal problem, but may be based solely on the facts. This considerably facilitates the process of claiming protection concerning the social rights guaranteed by the charter.[177] Similar to the views issued by the universal human rights treaty bodies, the committee's decisions are not "judgements", but their influence on member states' domestic law and practice appears to have considerable potential, because the committee not only confines itself to checking whether a state has introduced into its legal system provisions conferring certain rights, but is also interested in determining whether these rights can be effectively exercised.[178]

176 Council of Europe, "Additional Protocol to the European Social Charter Providing for a System of Collective Complaints, Strasbourg, 9 November 1995" (European Treaty Series No. 158), https://www.coe.int/en/web/conventions/full-list?module=treaty-detail&treatynum=158.

177 Macin Wujczyk, "Procedura Skarg Zbiorowych Jako Instrument Ochrony Praw Socjalnych [The Collective Complaints Procedure as an Instrument of Protection of Social Rights]", in *Europejska Karta Społeczna: Wyzwania i Możliwości 25. Rocznica Przystąpienia Polski Do Rady Europy [The European Social Charter: Challenges and Opportunities 25th Anniversary of Poland's Membership of the Council of Europe] Edited by Lesław Nawacki, Anna Szałek, Marcin Wujczyk* (Warsaw, 2016), 155.

178 See more: Council of Europe/ECSR, "Rules of the European Committee of Social Rights, Amended during the 328th Session on 6 July 2022" (Council of

The human rights treaty bodies are also competent to consider the reports that state parties are obliged to submit periodically on steps taken to implement the provisions of a relevant treaty. They review these reports, identify issues of concern and make "concluding observations." In the case of periodic reports, these concluding observations issued to state parties should be the starting point for identifying the issues to be included in the report, as committees examine the progress and challenges faced by the state parties in implementing earlier recommendations.

Prior to a state submitting its report for evaluation, the relevant committee sends the government a "List of Issues" or "List of Issues Prior to Reporting" according to the simplified procedure,[179] to which the report should be dedicated. Theoretically, if the list included some issues related to the specific situation of older persons, including older migrants, this could have a positive impact on the states' awareness and, consequently, compliance with their obligations under the treaties.

At the European level, the reporting procedure is set out in Part IV of the 1961 European Social Charter as amended by the 1991 Turin Protocol,[180] which is broader in coverage than the universal system and has the potential to improve the enforcement of social rights at a domestic level.

The reports submitted by state parties are analysed by the ESCR, which then decides whether the national situations described there comply with the charter. State parties report annually on provisions relating to one of four thematic groups. The key group for older persons is the group covering the states' obligations relating to health, social security, social protection

---

Europe, 2022), https://www.coe.int/en/web/european-social-charter/ingos-engagement-with-ecsr#{%2257676066 %22:[4],%2258046116 %22:[1]}.

179 Inter-Committee Technical Working Group, "Harmonized Guidelines on Reporting under the International Human Rights Treaties, Including Guidelines on a Common Core Document and Treaty-Specific Documents, Report of the Inter-Committee Technical Working Group", 2006, https://digitallibrary.un.org/record/600446; UN Secretary General, "Compilation of Guidelines on the Form and Content of Reports to Be Submitted by States Parties to the International Human Rights Treaties Report of the Secretary-General", 2009, https://digitallibrary.un.org/record/600446.

180 Council of Europe, "Protocol Amending the European Social Charter, Turin, 21 October 1991 (European Treaty Series – No. 142).

and the right to protection from poverty and social exclusion, which older migrants may experience. The committee's conclusions are not binding, but they may affect the member states' jurisprudence, law and practice.[181] They certainly contribute to raising the awareness of both the authorities and other entities involved in reporting.

Any review of the possibilities for using human rights machinery to encourage states to respect, protect, and uphold the rights of older persons, especially those who are vulnerable, should consider the potential of inquiry procedures. The main idea of this mechanism is to investigate grave and systematic violations of human rights. Its main advantages are flexibility, confidentiality and the fact that it does not require the exhaustion of domestic remedies. In Europe, the inquiry procedure set out in the European Convention for the Prevention of Torture and Inhuman or Degrading Treatment or Punishment of 1987[182] follows the first-established inquiry mechanism under the UN Convention against Torture and Other Cruel, Inhuman or Degrading Treatment or Punishment of 1984 (UN),[183] supplemented by the Optional Protocol of 2002 (UN).[184] Apart from the Committee Against Torture ("CAT"), there are five other committees empowered to conduct inquiries: CEDAW, CED, CRPD, CESCR and CRC.

181 Andrzej Marian Świątkowski and Macin Wujczyk, "Karta Praw Społecznych Rady Europy Jako Szansa Ustanowienia Jednolitej Koncepcji Obywatelstwa Unii Europejskiej [The Council of Europe's Charter of Social Rights as an Opportunity to Establish a Uniform Concept of European Union Citizenship]", *Roczniki Administracji i Prawa* XVI, No. 2 (2016): 433, http://cejsh.icm.edu.pl/cejsh/element/bwmeta1.element.desklight-f847bd20-3aff-4a65-8de4-a11fa6747b78.

182 Council of Europe, "European Convention for the Prevention of Torture and Inhuman or Degrading Treatment or Punishment, Strasbourg 26 November 1987" (European Treaty Series – No. 126,), https://www.coe.int/en/web/conventions/full-list?module=treaty-detail&treatynum=035.

183 United Nations, "Convention against Torture and Other Cruel, Inhuman or Degrading Treatment or Punishment, New York, 10 December 1984", (UNTS, Vol. 1465, p. 85).

184 United Nations, "Optional Protocol to the Convention against Torture and Other Cruel, Inhuman or Degrading Treatment or Punishment, New York, 18 December 2002", (UNTS 2006, vol. 2375, p. 237), https://treaties.un.org/Pages/ViewDetails.aspx?src=TREATY&mtdsg_no=IV-3-a&chapter=4&clang=_en.

Potentially, such procedures could be concerned with cases of older forced migrants in detention (e.g. at borders) or in closed centres for people seeking protection or in deportation detention. The Independent Expert, in her thematic report on the deprivation of liberty in older age, raises the issue of immigration-related detention, noting that border-enforcement settings generally lack the capacity for individualised assessments of the needs of detainees. Meanwhile, intersectional approaches are needed to assess necessity and proportionality when making decisions about the detention of older persons. Hence, detained migrants who are usually fleeing persecution, generalised violence, conflict, economic insecurity and threats to their lives, may experience trauma in those settings. She also notes that the lack of studies and data collection on immigration-related detention of older migrants leads to inappropriate practices and inadequate policies and laws concerning older migrants and asylum seekers, ending up with a higher risk of age-based discrimination and violence.[185]

In addition, the system of the Human Rights Council Special Procedures should also be taken into account, as this is a central element of the United Nations human rights machinery covering all human rights. A strong point of this system is that states are subject to it not because treaties bind them, but because they belong to an international community within the framework of the UN. The Special Procedures may undoubtedly improve the understanding of human rights and the identification of sources of unequal treatment as the Special Procedures Mandate Holders are guided in their actions by the Universal Declaration of Human Rights and soft law documents, which are crucial for categories of people who are not protected by a specific treaty, like older persons. They are independent experts who operate in dialogue with the relevant government authorities and cooperate with civil society organisations and other stakeholders.[186]

185 UN Independent Expert, "Report of the Independent Expert on the Enjoyment of All Human Rights by Older Persons 'Older Persons Deprived of Liberty', 13 September 2022, A/HRC/51/27" (United Nations General Assembly, 2022), paras. 51–52, https://www.ohchr.org/en/documents/thematic-reports/ahrc5127-older-persons-deprived-liberty-report-independent-expert.

186 Human Rights Council, "Code of Conduct for Special Procedures Mandate-Holders of the Human Rights Council. A/HCR/RES/5/2.", 2007.

Certainly, the activity of the Independent Expert on the enjoyment of all human rights by older persons is crucial for this study, as this body plays a principal role in including older persons' rights in the international debate. The Independent Expert publishes thematic reports and statements raising general awareness about older people in various circumstances and their rights. Conducting "country visits", the Independent Expert advises governments on their national legislation, policies, regulatory frameworks, institutions and practices in seeking to identify best practices and gaps in the implementation of existing human rights law. Finally, the Independent Expert may intervene in particular cases due to received communications.[187] For example, in a 2023 report on a visit to the Dominican Republic, the Independent Expert, Claudia Mahler, called on the authorities to grant older migrants access to social security and healthcare. Moreover, she stressed that the environmental disaster response must support older persons in vulnerable situations, older migrants and undocumented older persons.[188] The previous Independent Expert, Rosa Kornfeld Matte, in a report on a visit to Austria in 2015, also mentioned "older migrants," encouraging the government to take further measures to reduce poverty among older persons, including older women and older migrants, and to ensure equal access to social care and services and adequate and accessible information about the services available.[189]

It is certainly the case that the independent experts have addressed many issues that directly or indirectly affect older migrants, but this category of

187 Felice D. Gaer, "Picking and Choosing? Country Visits by Thematic Special Procedures", in *The United Nations Special Procedures System*, ed. Aoife Nolan, Rosa Freedman, and Thérèse Murphy (Brill | Nijhoff, 2017), 88, https://dokumen.pub/the-united-nations-special-procedures-system-1nbsped-9789004304703-9789004304697.html ; Human Rights Council, "Code of Conduct for Special Procedures Mandate-Holders of the Human Rights Council. A/HCR/RES/5/2."

188 Independent Expert, "Report of the Independent Expert on the Enjoyment of All Human Rights by Older Persons, Visit to the Dominican Republic, A/HRC/54/26/Add.3", 2023, paras. 78 and 92, https://uhri.ohchr.org/en/document/56705239-99b7-4c9d-ac49-ecf7d3487b5f.

189 Human Rights Council, "Report of the Independent Expert on the Enjoyment of All Human Rights by Older Persons, Visit to Austria, A/HRC/30/43/Add.2", 2015, paras. 90-92, https://uhri.ohchr.org/en/document/242c199a-4c80-41ed-bc0e-b1e1c0b36d3c.

older people is explicitly mentioned in the reports. Similarly, migrants and older people are present in the reports of other mandate holders whose migration issues remain within their mandate, most notably the Special Rapporteur on the human rights of migrants and the Special Rapporteur on the human rights of internally displaced persons. It is noteworthy that the recent report of the Special Rapporteur on the human rights of internally displaced persons, Cecilia Jimenez-Damary, on her visit to Japan, indicated a failure to recognise the problems and inequalities faced by older persons displaced by the Fukushima nuclear power plant disaster. She recommended that the Japanese authorities enable older people to make decisions on their return to their former residences. However, it turns out that older returnees face obstacles in some areas related to limited local services, which is why she called for relevant measures to be taken in this regard.[190]

Another Human Rights Council procedure is the Universal Periodic Review (UPR), which involves a review of the human rights records of all UN member states. The review of achievements and shortcomings in a state's respect for human rights and performance of its obligations is carried out periodically by other states. During recent UPR cycles, older persons' rights have become a more and more frequent topic of review. States are engaged in dialogue on the rights of migrants, and increasingly on the situation of older people. However, there have been no questions or recommendations about older migrants. That is why the recommendation from Malaysia to Austria to take further measures to reduce poverty among older persons, particularly older women and older migrants, is exceptional.[191]

---

190 Special Rapporteur on the human rights of internally displaced persons, "Report of the Special Rapporteur on the Human Rights of Internally Displaced Persons, Cecilia Jimenez-Damary, on Her Visit to Japan, para. 95, A/HRC/53/35/Add.1", 2023, https://uhri.ohchr.org/en/document/56705239-99b7-4c9d-ac49-ecf7d3487b5f.

191 Human Rights Council, "Report of the Working Group on the Universal Periodic Review, Austria, 9 April 2021, A/HRC/47/12", 2021, para. 139, https://uhri.ohchr.org/en/document/6fb70583-70d1-49b7-b2b7-2d2a7fd448fe.

The list of human rights mechanisms is longer.[192] There are other Human Rights Council mechanisms, including the complaints procedure established by Resolution 5/1 of 2007,[193] the entirely confidential UNESCO complaint procedure which is based on dialogue with governments,[194] and the International Labour Organization reporting and complaints procedures.[195]

It can be assumed that in each of the briefly outlined procedures, there is space to include older migrants in human rights monitoring and dialogue with states. However, it is important to be aware that all of these procedures must be accepted by states, while, states are not always willing to cooperate with international human rights bodies, and sometimes their actions have no substance.[196] In addition, some mechanisms, mainly the UPR, are intensely politicised, which has resulted in their dilution.[197] Finally, there are no guarantees that states will implement all the judgements, views, observations or recommendations.[198] Taking steps of an inclusive nature

---

192 See more: Mikołajczyk, *Social Inclusion for Older Persons and Human Rights Law. The Potential for Universal and European Instruments*, 173–76.

193 Human Rights Council, "Institution-Building of the United Nations Human Rights Council Resolution A/HRC/RES/5/1, 18 June 2007", https://ap.ohchr.org/documents/dpage_e.aspx?si=a/hrc/res/5/1.

194 UNESCO, "Decisions Adopted by the Executive Board at Its 104th Session, Paris, 24 April-9 June 1978" (UNESCO, 1978), https://unesdoc.unesco.org/ark:/48223/pf0000028409.locale=en.

195 *Handbook of Procedures Relating to International Labour Conventions and Recommendations International Labour Standards Department International Labour*, Rev. ed. 2012 (Geneva: ILO, 2012).

196 Rhona K M Smith, "States of Denial: Rationalising UK Government Responses to UN Special Procedures", *Human Rights Law Review* 21, No. 2 (12 March 2021): 458–74, https://doi.org/10.1093/hrlr/ngaa049.

197 Rosa Freedman, "The Human Rights Council", in *The UN and Human Rights: A Critical Appraisal*, ed. Frédéric Mégret and Philip Alston, Second edition (New York: Oxford University Press, 2019), 202–3; Rosa Freedman and Jacob Mchangama, "Expanding or Diluting Human Rights?: The Proliferation of United Nations Special Procedures Mandates", *Human Rights Quarterly* 38, No. 1 (2016): 164–93, https://doi.org/10.1353/hrq.2016.0012.

198 Committee of Ministers, "Supervision of the Execution of Judgments and Decisions of the European Court of Human Rights. 14th Annual Report of the Committee of Ministers" (Strasbourg, March 2021), https://edoc.coe.int/en/european-convention-on-human-rights/9725-supervision-of-the-execution-of-judgments-and-decisions-of-the-european-court-of-human-rights-2020-14th-annual-report-of-the-committee-of-ministers.html; Michael O'Flaherty, "The

for older migrants in migration and social policies is met with reluctance by states, as migration is a political topic, often used in election campaigns. At the same time, taking steps that place a financial burden on budgets, e.g. medical care for non-nationals, can also be exploited politically. Migration issues and the "defence of nationals from strangers" is a catch-all for populist governments.[199]

On the other hand, procedures can work on a "drop drills the rock" basis. Despite the invisibility of older migrants in the core human rights treaties, they may raise the awareness of states and other stakeholders and thereby improve the visibility of older migrants internationally and improve their behaviour at a national level in various sectors of life. However, clearer and more precise instructions should be sought in specialised international law dedicated to migrations and older persons.

Concluding Observations of United Nations Human Rights Treaty Bodies", *Human Rights Law Review* 6, No. 1 (2006): 27–52; Ulfstein, "Individual Complaints"; UN Secretary General, "Status of the Human Rights Treaty Body System. Report of the Secretary-General, A/74/643" (United Nations General Assembly, January 2020), https://digitallibrary.un.org/record/3849276; Xuelian Zhang, "On the Concluding Observations of the United Nations Human Rights Treaty Bodies", *Journal of Human Rights* 18, No. 3 (2019): 351–64.

199 Barbara Mikołajczyk and Mariusz Jagielski, " 'Good Change' and Migration Policy in Poland: In a Trap of Democracy", in *Migrants' Rights, Populism and Legal Resilience in Europe*, ed. Vladislava Stoyanova and Stijn Smet, 1st ed. (Cambridge University Press, 2022), 237, https://doi.org/10.1017/9781009040396.014.

4. Lex specialis

4.1. Older voluntary migrants

As argued above, the group of voluntary migrants consists of various subgroups, not usually considered vulnerable. They should enjoy the protection of their rights under general human rights law, including the right to social security and a proper standard, as set out in the Universal Declaration of Human Rights (Articles 22 and 25) and the International Covenant on Economic, Social and Cultural Rights (Article 9). The covenant imposes obligations on states regarding "…. the right of everyone to an adequate standard of living for himself and his family, including adequate food, clothing and housing, and to the continuous improvement of living conditions…" (Article 11), as well as "the right of everyone to the enjoyment of the highest attainable standard of physical and mental health…" (Article 12).

However, as indicated in previous parts of this study, even voluntary older migrants, in certain situations, face obstacles to the exercise of their rights as they are invisible in general human rights treaties. The question must, therefore, be asked whether the branches of international law dedicated to migrants and older persons provide sufficient protection for older migrants.

A particular subcategory of migrants are migrant workers. As noted above, they also enjoy their own global convention – the International Convention on the Protection of the Rights of All Migrant Workers and Members of Their Families, adopted in 1990. However, despite the fact that it prohibits age discrimination, it does not contain any precise provisions referring to older migrant workers and retired migrants. However, to some extent, Article 27 can be a basis for establishing the states' obligations in the "retirement and pensions sphere." It stipulates "with respect to social security, migrant workers and members of their families shall enjoy in the State of employment the same treatment granted to nationals in so far as they fulfil the requirements provided for by the applicable legislation of that State and the applicable bilateral and multilateral treaties. The competent authorities of the State of origin and the State of employment can at any time establish the necessary arrangements to determine the modalities of application of this norm."

It is easy to note that states enjoy a certain margin of appreciation in this sphere and they are allowed to regulate these matters in bilateral agreements. The Committee on the Protection of the Rights of All Migrant Workers and Members, as of now, has not provided any specific guidance in this area.

Meanwhile, when interpreting the convention, in its General Comment No. 5 of 2021 on migrants' rights to liberty and freedom from arbitrary detention and their connection with other human rights, the committee formulated the principle that there should be no detention of migrant workers or members of their families if they are in vulnerable situations. According to the committee, states should avoid detaining migrants with special needs, including older persons. The committee's interpretation is crucial, as undocumented migrants are detained in many states without there being any alternatives to detention.[200]

The recent universal milestone document relating to migration – the Global Compact for Safe, Orderly and Regular Migration, adopted by the UN General Assembly in 2018 – calls upon states to establish comprehensive policies and develop partnerships that provide migrants in situations of vulnerability, regardless of their migration status, with necessary support at all stages of migration, through identification and assistance, as well as the protection of their human rights, in particular in cases related to various groups at risk, including older persons. One of the Global Compact's objectives is to establish or maintain non-discriminatory national social protection systems, including social protection floors for nationals and migrants, and to take relevant measures to address the difficulties of older persons in accessing social protection.

The Global Compact is not a legally binding political act, but it urges states to perform their obligations arising from international treaties

200 Committee on the Protection of the Rights of All Migrant Workers and Members of Their Families, "General Comment No. 5 (2021) on Migrants' Rights to Liberty and Freedom from Arbitrary Detention and Their Connection with Other Human Rights, 21 July 2021, CMW/C/GC/5.", https://www.ohchr.org/en/documents/general-comments-and-recommendations/general-comment-no-5-2021-migrants-rights-liberty.

adopted in the UN forum, regional commitments and international labour law, including the International Labour Organization the Social Protection Floors Recommendation. The UN General Assembly calls on states to: "a) Establish or maintain non-discriminatory national social protection systems, including social protection floors for nationals and migrants, in line with the ILO Social Protection Floors Recommendation, 2012 (No. 202); (b) Conclude reciprocal bilateral, regional or multilateral social security agreements on the portability of earned benefits for migrant workers at all skills levels, referring to applicable social protection floors in the respective States and applicable social security entitlements and provisions, such as pensions, health care or other earned benefits, or integrate such provisions into other relevant agreements, such as those on long-term and temporary labour migration."[201]

There are also other ILO instruments that can certainly be taken into account when analysing the protection of older migrant workers. One of them is the Social Security (Minimum Standards) Convention 1952 (No. 102), which establishes the principle of equality of treatment between national and non-national residents of countries of employment, although it does also allow for exceptions, including in the area of contributory social schemes.[202] Article 5 of the Equality of Treatment (Social Security) Convention of 1962 establishes the principle of the provision of benefits abroad, including old-age, invalidity and survivors' benefits, death grants and employment injury pensions. However, this provision is applied only in the case of nationals of another state that has also ratified the convention, which, as of January 2024, included 38 state-parties.[203]

201 UN General Assembly, "Resolution Adopted by the General Assembly. Global Compact for Safe, Orderly and Regular Migration, 19 December 2018, A/RES/73/195", para. 38, https://documents.un.org/doc/undoc/gen/n18/451/99/pdf/n1845199.pdfOpenElement.

202 ILO, "The Social Security (Minimum Standards) Convention (No. 102)", 4 June 1952, https://www.ilo.org/dyn/normlex/en/f?p=NORMLEXPUB:12100:0::NO:12100:P12100_INSTRUMENT_ID:312247:NO.

203 ILO, "Convention No. 118, Equality of Treatment (Social Security), 6 June 1962," https://www.ilo.org/dyn/normlex/en/f?p=NORMLEXPUB:12100:0::NO::P12100_INSTRUMENT_ID:312263.

The Invalidity, Old-Age and Survivors' Benefits Convention adopted in 1967 and ratified by 17 states, refers to "all residents", so it might be assumed that it also protects migrants, though the convention does not refer to the portability of benefits and summing years of contribution or employment in various states of residence.[204]

The notion of "portability" appears in ILO documents adopted in this century, including the Multilateral Framework on Labour Migration of 2006, which contains non-binding principles and guidelines for a rights-based approach to labour migration. It encourages states to enter into bilateral, regional and multilateral agreements to provide social security coverage and benefits, as well as the portability of social security entitlements, to both regular migrant workers and, as appropriate, to migrant workers in irregular situations. It also indicates the good practices of some states showing that migrant workers using official channels receive relevant training and full information pre-departure pension plans.[205] Another example is the ILO's guide for policymakers and practitioners providing ways of expanding social protection for migrant workers and forced migrants.[206]

Meanwhile, only five states have ratified a treaty containing a whole section on the maintenance of rights and the provision of benefits, including pensions and old-age and survivors' cash benefits abroad, also covering migrant workers and refugees. This is the Maintenance of Social Security Rights Convention, 1982 (No. 157), which in common with other ILO treaties allows states to regulate these matters by separate agreements.[207]

---

204 ILO, "Convention No128 – on Invalidity, Old-Age and Survivors' Benefits Convention", 7 June 1967, https://www.ilo.org/dyn/normlex/en/f?p=NORMLEXPUB:12100:0::NO::P12100_INSTRUMENT_ID:312273.

205 Internationales Arbeitsamt, ed., *ILO Multilateral Framework on Labour Migration: Non-Binding Principles and Guidelines for a Rights-Based Approach to Labour Migration* (Geneva: International Labour Office, 2006), 50.

206 *Extending Social Protection to Migrant Workers, Refugees and Their Families.*

207 ILO, "Maintenance of Social Security Rights Convention, (No. 157)", 2 June 1982, https://www.ilo.org/dyn/normlex/en/f?p=NORMLEXPUB:12100:0::NO:12100:P12100_INSTRUMENT_ID:312302:NO.

It should be stressed that the ILO[208] and the UN encourage states to conclude bilateral labour agreements as useful tools for extending the rights of migrant workers by providing memoranda of understanding and models of such treaties.[209] Following this trend, the European Union and the Mediterranean countries are attempting to solve the problems that exist regarding social security scheme coordination through the negotiation of bilateral agreements in the framework of the European Neighbourhood Policy.[210]

In the ILO forum, instruments protecting migrants have been adopted since its inception. One can even speak of a specialised part of international labour law adopted in the form of this organisation, which consists of numerous conventions and recommendations. In the context of this study, a convention from 1935 on the Maintenance of Migrants' Pension Rights deserves special attention, as it stipulates, among other things, that everyone, regardless of their nationality, who belonged to insurance institutions of two or more ILO member states will have their insurance periods aggregated by each of the institutions concerned.[211] This convention, which is now almost a century old, seems to have come closest to dealing with the problems of a certain proportion of older migrants. However, only twelve countries are parties to this convention.

Meanwhile, the ILO Convention Concerning Migration for Employment (Revised) does not refer explicitly to older workers, except for a provision allowing states to adopt special regulations concerning allowances

---

208 For example in the e. g. in the 1949 Migration for Employment Recommendation (Revised) (No. 86) https://www.ilo.org/dyn/normlex/en/f?p=NORMLEXPUB:12100:0::NO:12100:P12100_INSTRUMENT_ID:312424:NO.

209 United Nations Network on Migration, "Guidance on Bilateral Labour Migration Agreements" (United Nations, 2022), https://www.ilo.org/global/topics/labour-migration/publications/WCMS_837529/lang--en/index.htm. *Extending Social Protection to Migrant Workers, Refugees and Their Families*, 104.

210 European Economic and Social Committee., *Coordination of Social Security Schemes between the European Union and Euromed Countries :Study.* (LU: Publications Office, 2016), 16, https://data.europa.eu/doi/10.2864/94071.

211 ILO, "Maintenance of Migrants' Pension Rights Convention No. 48, 4 June 1935", https://www.ilo.org/dyn/normlex/en/f?p=NORMLEXPUB:12100:0::NO:12100:P12100_INSTRUMENT_ID:312193:NO.

paid to people who do not meet the contribution conditions prescribed for the award of a regular pension (Article 6).[212] Another treaty referring to migrant workers – the Convention Concerning Migrations in Abusive Conditions and the Promotion of Equality of Opportunity and Treatment of Migrant Workers of 1975 – also fails to mention older workers, pensions or other old-age benefits. However, it does stipulate that states' obligations in this area should be interpreted from the general clause stating that "Each Member for which this Convention is in force undertakes to respect the basic human rights of all migrant workers."[213]

The European regional international law,[214] including the European Convention on the Legal Status of Migrant Workers of 1977,[215] is also silent on older members of this category of migrants. In a very general way, it refers to the obligation on states to ensure they treat migrant workers and members of their families equally with their nationals regarding social

212 ILO, "Migration for Employment Convention (Revised), No. 97, 8 June 1949", https://www.ilo.org/dyn/normlex/en/f?p=NORMLEXPUB:55:0::NO::P55_TYPE,P55_LANG,P55_DOCUMENT,P55_NODE:CON,en,C097,/Document.

213 ILO, "Convention Concerning Migrations in Abusive Conditions and the Promotion of Equality of Opportunity and Treatment of Migrant Workers, No. 143, 4 June 1975", https://www.ilo.org/dyn/normlex/en/f?p=NORMLEXPUB:55:0::NO::P55_TYPE,P55_LANG,P55_DOCUMENT,P55_NODE:CON,en,C097,/Document.

214 Certainly, various instruments on migrant workers have been adopted in the other regional fora, for example, "the Inter-American Program for the Promotion and Protection of the Human Rights of Migrants, Including Migrant Workers and their Families". Other examples are agreements on social security, covering also of old-age pensions and other benefits concluded in the framework of the Caribbean Community, MERCOSUR (Mercado Común del Sur), Inter-African Conference on Social Insurance, and Economic Community of West African States. Worth indicating are also initiatives leading to the adoption of the Ibero-American Multilateral Agreement on Social Security of 2016, and the Unified Law on Insurance Protection Extension for Citizens of Gulf Cooperation Council States Working outside Their Countries in Any of the Council Member States adopted in 2006. As the ILO' study noted, they usually needs taking further steps which face many obstacles due to the administrative complexity and economic challenges. See: ILO Multilateral agreements, https://www.social-protection.org/gimi/gess/ShowWiki.action?wiki.wikiId=938

215 Council of Europe, "The European Convention on the Legal Status of Migrant Workers, 24 November 1977", (Council of Europe Treaty Series – No. 93).

security. It refers to national legislation and bilateral or multilateral treaties that regulate these matters (Article 18). The treaty has been ratified by 11 of the 46 Council of Europe member states. In this situation, the mentioned Revised European Charter (RESC) and its Article 19, setting out the rights of migrant workers and their families to protection and assistance, should be taken into account, in connection with Article 23 proclaiming the right of older persons to social protection, as well as Articles 30, containing the right to protection against poverty and social exclusion and 31 on the right to housing. It is clear from this that these provisions are essential for older migrants, but, unfortunately, not all the CoE member states are parties to the RESC.[216] Moreover, the charter allows states to select certain obligations to be bound by due to the *à la carte* system,[217] and it turns out that the above-mentioned provisions are the least frequently chosen by the states parties.

Some guidelines for states in the areas that are crucial for older voluntary migrants come from the Council of Europe's soft law. The CoE Parliamentary Assembly (PACE) Recommendation 1619 (2003)1 – "Rights of elderly migrants" – called on the CoE member states to develop coherent and comprehensive policies to address the situation of older migrants through such things as providing social protection, ensuring the transferability of full pension rights for migrant workers, wherever they decide to take up residence, adapting the existing structures for the provision of healthcare and assistance to make them culturally appropriate, facilitating access to healthcare and assistance services through the provision of free interpretation upon demand for older migrants, in the event that they are not able to communicate effectively in the language of the host country.[218]

---

216 35 parties in March 2024.

217 Israel Doron and Gerard Quinn, *Against Ageism and Towards Active Social Citizenship for Older Persons The Current Use and Future Potential of the European Social Charter* (Strasbourg: Council of Europe, 2021), https://rm.coe.int/against-ageism-and-towards-active-social-citizenship-for-older-persons/1680a3f5da.

218 Council of Europe, "Parliamentary Assembly Recommendation "Rights of Elderly Migrants" 1619 (2003), 9 August 2003", https://assembly.coe.int/nw/xml/XRef/Xref-XML2HTML-en.asp?fileid=17137&lang=en.

Regarding irregular migrants, in its Resolution 1509 (2006), PACE indicated that the detention of irregular migrants should be used only as a last resort, and not for an excessive period. In the case of vulnerable people the immigration detention should be avoided whenever possible. In addition, emergency healthcare should be available to irregular migrants. That is why PACE calls for governments to provide more holistic healthcare, taking into account, in particular, the specific needs of vulnerable groups, including older persons.[219]

Among the recommendations issued by the CoE Committee of Ministers in migrant matters,[220] it is worth noting Recommendation CM/Rec(2011)5, which called on member states to reduce the risk of vulnerability to older migrants and improve their welfare.[221]

Recommendation CM/Rec(2014)2 of the Committee of Ministers to member states on the promotion of human rights of older persons does not refer to older migrants of any kind, but it does stipulate that older persons must be able to enjoy their rights and freedoms without discrimination on any grounds, calling on the CoE member states to take effective measures to prevent multiple discrimination of older persons. The part of the recommendation related to employment and social protection is an important guidance for states as it proclaims that older persons should receive appropriate resources enabling them to have an adequate standard of living and participate in public, economic, social and cultural life.[222] This recommendation is not usually associated with older migrants. In the first overview of the implementation of the recommendation, only Finland reported that

219 Council of Europe Parliamentary Assembly, "Resolution 1509 (2006) on Human Rights of Irregular Migrants", 2006, https://assembly.coe.int/nw/xml/xref/xref-xml2html-en.asp?fileid=17456.

220 See the list https://www.coe.int/t/democracy/migration/ressources/recommendations-resolutions_en.asp.

221 Committee of Ministers, "Council of Europe Committee of Recommendation CM/Rec(2011)5 of the Committee of Ministers to Member States on Reducing the Risk of Vulnerability of Elderly Migrants and Improving Their Welfare", 2011, https://www.coe.int/t/democracy/migration/ressources/recommendations-resolutions_en.asp.

222 Committee of Ministers, "Recommendation CM/Rec(2014)2 Adopted by the Committee of Ministers of the Council of Europe on 19 February 2014".

municipalities and civil society organisations had run projects to promote the integration of immigrants aged over 65.[223]

Within the European Union, the situation of migrants depends primarily on their nationality. Citizens of the EU, as well as of Iceland, Liechtenstein, Norway and Switzerland (the EU+), benefit from free movement. In turn, after Brexit, the status of UK citizens results from the UK-EU Withdrawal Agreement.[224] The EU law on free movement also covers coordination schemes, the transfer of old-age benefits, and survivors' pensions among the EU Member States.[225] The EU+ nationals and their family members who are or have been insured in one of these countries are covered by coordination rules in this area. These rules are also applied to third-country nationals, as well as stateless persons and refugees who are legally residing in these states. For example, third-country nationals possessing long-term resident status enjoy equal treatment with nationals of an EU Member State, including social security, social assistance and social protection as defined by national law.[226]

---

223 Steering Committee for Human Rights, "Steering Committee for Human Rights, Report on the Implementation of the Committee of Ministers' Recommendation CM/Rec (2014) 2 on the Promotion of Human Rights of Older Persons Adopted by the CDDH at Its 90th Meeting (27–30 November 2018), CDDH(2018)R90 Addendum 07/01/2019" (Council of Europe, 2019), 6, https://rm.coe.int/steering-committee-for-human-rights-cddh-cddh-report-on-the-implementa/1680906e2f.

224 "Agreement on the withdrawal of the United Kingdom of Great Britain and Northern Ireland from the European Union and the European Atomic Energy Community," (O. J. C 384I, 12.11.2019, p. 1–177), https://eur-lex.europa.eu/legal-content/EN/TXT/?uri=CELEX%3A12019W/TXT%2802%29.

225 European Union, "Regulation (EC) No. 883/2004 of the European Parliament and of the Council of 29 April 2004 on the Coordination of Social Security Systems" (O. J. L 166, 30.4.2004 p. 1–126, 2004), https://eur-lex.europa.eu/eli/reg/2004/883/oj; European Union; European Union, "Directive 2014/50/EU of the European Parliament and of the Council of 16 April 2014 on Minimum Requirements for Enhancing Worker Mobility between Member States by Improving the Acquisition and Preservation of Supplementary Pension Rights" (O. J. L 128, 30.4. 2014, p. 1–7), https://eur-lex.europa.eu/eli/dir/2014/50/oj.

226 European Union, "Council Directive 2003/109/EC of 25 November 2003 Concerning the Status of Third-Country Nationals Who Are Long-Term

Meanwhile, securing the rights of migrants in an irregular situation remains a constant challenge in the EU.[227] The problems of older irregular migrants cannot, therefore, be expected to be dealt with in a special way under EU law. It is already a great challenge for them to exercise the fundamental rights contained in the ECHR and the Charter of Fundamental Rights.

The situation of older migrants should also be analysed from the perspective of international law on older persons. As mentioned earlier, no convention on the rights of older persons has yet been adopted in the general international forum.

The Inter-American Convention on Protecting the Human Rights of Older Persons of 2015, which may be perceived as a guide for a future universal convention, contains a non-discrimination clause in its Article 5, calling on state-parties to develop their policies, plans, and legislation on ageing and old age-specific approaches for older persons who are vulnerable and victims of multiple discrimination. Significantly, "migrants" are itemised among these vulnerable groups. Meanwhile, in the area of social security, the convention refers state parties to other bilateral and regional agreements in this area.[228] Under such an arrangement, older migrants may be treated differently, depending on the will of the states reflected in agreements, if any such agreements have been concluded at all. It seems that a future universal convention could set some minimum standards in this respect. Meanwhile, the Protocol to the African Charter on Human and Peoples' Rights on the Rights of Older Persons does not refer to migrants, at all.

Thus, the treaty law relating to older people, including older migrants, is extremely modest. However, as argued above, this does not mean that states

---

Residents, O. J. L 16, 23.1.2004, pp. 44–53" (O. J. L 16, 21.1.2003, pp. 44–53) Article 11, https://eur-lex.europa.eu/legal-content/EN/TXT/?uri=celex%3A32003L0109.

227 European Union Agency for Fundamental Rights., *Fundamental Rights of Migrants in an Irregular Situation in the European Union: Comparative Report.* (LU: Publications Office, 2011), https://data.europa.eu/doi/10.2811/19312; Fox-Ruhs and Ruhs, "The Fundamental Rights of Irregular Migrant Workers in the EU".

228 See Article 17 in the Annex. p. 135

do not have obligations towards them, stemming primarily from treaties that protect the rights of all people. In such situations, soft law documents provide essential interpretive guidance for determining the obligations of states. However, concerning voluntary migrants, the soft law documents are also constrained. For example, the ILO's Recommendation on older workers of 1980,[229] which, despite not being legally binding, is perceived as a key document on older persons adopted in the ILO's forum, does not touch on migration aspects.

The Vienna Action Plan on Ageing of 1982 does not mention older persons in a migratory situation.[230] The United Nations Principles for Older Persons of 1991[231] is a document of unique importance, as it sets out the principles of independence, participation, care, self-fulfilment and dignity of older persons in each life situation. However, this document of manifesto nature certainly does not indicate any vulnerable situations.[232]

The Madrid International Plan of Action on Ageing (MIPAA) and the Political Declaration adopted at the Second World Assembly on Ageing in April 2002, as endorsed by the General Assembly in Resolution 57/167,[233]

229 International Labour Organization, "Older Workers Recommendation, 1980 (No. 162) Adopted on 3 June 1980 by the General Conference of the International Labour Organisation", 1980, https://www.ilo.org/dyn/normlex/en/f?p=NORMLEXPUB:12100:0::NO::P12100_ILO_CODE:R162.

230 United Nations, "Vienna International Plan of Action on Ageing, Report of the World Assembly on Ageing, Vienna, 26 July–6 August 1982. General Assembly Resolution 37/51, Question on Ageing", (United Nations, 1982), https://www.un.org/esa/socdev/ageing/documents/Resources/VIPEE-English.pdf.

231 UN General Assembly, "United Nations Principles for Older Persons Adopted 16 December 1991, A/RES/46/91", https://undocs.org/A/RES/46/91.

232 However, worth noting is that the Inter-American Program within the OAS for the Promotion and Protection of the Human Rights of Migrants, Including Migrant Workers and their Families, adopted in 2005 by the General Assembly of the Organization of American States, invokes the Principles among sets of rules and principles for the interpretation of international obligations. Organization of American States, "Inter-American Program for the Promotion and Protection of the Human Rights of Migrants, Including Migrant Workers and Their Families, (June 7, 2005), AG/RES. 2141 (XXXV-O/05)", http://rialnet.org/sites/default/files/AG-RES_2141_XXXV-O-05_eng.pdf.

233 United Nations, "Madrid International Plan of Action on Ageing and the Political Declaration, Report of the Second World Assembly on Ageing, Madrid, 8–12 April 2002 (United Nations Publication, Sales No E.02.IV.4)",

is recognised as the most comprehensive achievement of the global international community in the protection of the rights of older people. Its main message is "building a society for all ages," and its specific guidelines focus on older persons' development, health and well-being into old age, along with ensuring enabling and supportive environments. Most importantly, the MIPAA is a long-term process with a follow-up mechanism requiring a systematic review of its implementation, distinguishing it from many other plans and declarations. The MIPAA identifies the problems of older migrants from rural to urban areas in developing countries, who often face a loss of social networks and suffer from the lack of support infrastructure in cities, which can lead to their marginalisation and exclusion, particularly if they are ill or disabled. In many (usually developing) countries, they lose economic autonomy and physical and social care from family members, who must earn their living outside the home. They experience poverty and living in crowded housing. Therefore, states should act in the area of integrating older migrants within their new communities. Following the MIPAA, the governments should, among others, take measures to support social networks for older migrants, assist them in sustaining economic and health security, create age–friendly housing and intergenerational environment, develop integration policies and programmes and remove linguistic and cultural barriers when providing public services to older migrants.[234]

Finally, in 2021, the UN Human Rights Council adopted the substantive resolution "Human Rights of Older Persons," which is recognised as an important step forward in advancing older people's rights and the fight against ageism and age-based discrimination worldwide.[235] The resolution reaffirms the obligation of all states to respect, protect and fulfil the human rights of older people. However, the resolution does not refer to migrants as vulnerable older persons. It does not devote much space to intersectional

---

2002, https://www.un.org/development/desa/ageing/madrid-plan-of-action-and-its-implementation.html.

234 United Nations, Objective 3, para. 34.

235 See e.g. the Age Platform's opinion https://www.age-platform.eu/rights-of-older-persons-substantive-resolution-adopted-by-un-council/; the GARROP statement https://rightsofolderpeople.org/the-first-ever-substantive-resolution-on-rights-of-older-persons-adopted-by-the-human-rights-council/

discrimination either, and certainly not in the context of migration, calling only for the collection of data on intersectional and multiple discrimination and emphasising that older women often face multiple and intersecting forms of discrimination as victims of violence, age or disability or on other grounds, which affects the enjoyment of their human rights.[236] Thus, it can be assumed that "other grounds" also include migration status, but it requires the awareness and goodwill of states and other stakeholders to that such discrimination. Indeed, older women are particularly vulnerable to discrimination, but certainly, states have obligations towards all persons under their jurisdiction, regardless of gender and resident status.

4.2. Older persons in forced migration

International law regarding forced migration does not really address the specific situation of older migrants. The mentioned Geneva Convention Relating to the Status of Refugees of 1951 and the 1967 New York Protocol fail to indicate older or other vulnerable refugees.[237] Only Article 23 of the convention sets out the principle of equality of treatment between nationals and refugees lawfully staying in a state party concerning public relief and assistance. Article 24 requires states to adopt relevant social security legislation, including old age provisions.

The Geneva Convention relates mainly to people who are persecuted due to their race, religion, nationality, membership in a particular social group, or political opinion. The recognition of refugee status is a declaratory act. A person is a refugee as soon as they meet the criteria contained in the definition of a refugee (Article 1 of the convention). This necessarily occurs before the time when refugee status is formally recognised, which is why people applying for refugee status should also be protected, particularly against *refoulement* (Article 33). In other areas, the situation of asylum

236 Human Rights Council, "Resolution Human Rights of Older Persons Adopted by the Human Rights Council on 7 October 2021, A/HRC/RES/48/3", 2021, Preamble, https://documents-dds-ny.un.org/doc/UNDOC/GEN/G21/287/79/PDF/G2128779.pdf?OpenElement.

237 United Nations, "Convention Relating to the Status of Refugees, 28 July 1951'; UNTS, https://Treaties.Un.Org/Doc/Publication/UNTS/Volume%20606/Volume-606-I-8791-English.Pdf".

seekers, whether or not they are going through the process of being granted international protection, is regulated by national laws (the EU law is an exception) as there is no treaty on the rights of i.e. those who have applied for protection in a foreign state.

The guidance provided by the soft law acts is very general. The UN Declaration on Territorial Asylum of 1967 aims primarily to confirm the human right to seek and enjoy asylum from persecution, as stipulated in Article 14 of the Universal Declaration of Human Rights, so it does not refer to various needs of people, including older persons, who are or should be granted protection.[238]

The Global Compact on Refugees of 2018,[239] a programmatic document outlining the international community's activities, makes minimal references to older refugees.[240] They are only mentioned, among many other groups, when calling on the adoption of a participatory approach to various vulnerable groups of refugees and in the context of the promotion of sports and cultural activities among them. This reference, however, does not address the more pressing needs of older refugees and asylum seekers.

Given such limited references to older refugees and asylum seekers in hard and soft refugee law, states and other stakeholders may seek guidance from UNHCR policy papers and states, for example: UNHCR's Policy on Older Refugees (2000) re-affirming support for the United Nations Principles for Older Persons and the International Plan of Action on Ageing,[241] Policy on Age, Gender and Diversity (2018),[242] the UNHCR

---

238 UN General Assembly, "Declaration on Territorial Asylum, 14 December 1967, A/RES/2312(XXII)", https://www.refworld.org/docid/3b00f05a2c.html.

239 UN General Assembly, "Global Compact on Refugees Adopted by the General Assembly Resolution, 17 December 2018 A/RES/73/151", 2018, https://globalcompactrefugees.org/sites/default/files/2019-12/Global%20compact%20on%20refugees%20EN.pdf.

240 See more: NGO Committee on Ageing, Geneva, "The Rights of Older Persons in the Global Compact on Refugees Submitted by the NGO Committee on Ageing, Geneva", 2018, https://ageingcommitteegeneva.org/resources/documents/.

241 UNHCR, "UNHCR's Policy on Older Refugees' (UNHCR, 19 April 2000), EC/50/SC/CRP.1."

242 UNHCR, "UNHCR Policy on Age, Gender and Diversity", 2018, https://www.refworld.org/docid/5bb628ea4.html.

Emergency Handbook – Older Persons (2020),[243] Working with Older Persons in Forced Displacement (2021).[244] All of these aim to make older persons more visible in the international agenda. For example, the first message of the UNHCR Emergency Handbook – Older Persons, addressed to the UNHCR staff and others assisting people "on the move" is, "Do not assume older persons are visible; actively identify them." Its main principles are participation, fairness, respect, autonomy and equality. They clearly touch on the essence of all older persons' rights and dignity. Unfortunately, these policy papers are certainly not binding.

On the other hand, Article 35 sec. 1 of the 1951 Convention Relating to the Status of Refugees, which refers to the cooperation of the national authorities with the United Nations, does not allow governments to ignore the UNHCR guidance. Article 35 sec. 1 stipulates that "the Contracting States undertake to co-operate with the Office of the United Nations High Commissioner for Refugees, or any other agency of the United Nations which may succeed it, in the exercise of its functions, and shall in particular facilitate its duty of supervising the application of the provisions of this Convention."

Walter Kälin indicates the authoritative character of the UNHCR handbooks, guidelines and statements. It does not mean that they are legally binding, but they cannot be ignored by states.[245]

The Council of Europe also acts using soft and practical instruments. It adopts action plans, including the newest Action Plan on Protecting Vulnerable Persons in the Context of Migration and Asylum in Europe

243 UNHCR, "Emergency Handbook. Older Persons".

244 UNHCR, "Working with Older Persons in Forced Displacement", 2021, https://www.refworld.org/cgi-bin/texis/vtx/rwmain?page=search&docid=4ee72aaf2&skip=0&query=need%20to%20know%20guidance%20older%20people&_gl=1*1i3b67o*_rup_ga*MTc4NjcwODA4My4xNzAzMjc3MTk5*_rup_ga_EVDQTJ4LMY*MTcwNjQ2MTg5MC4xNC4xLjE3MDY0NjIxNzYuMC4wLjA.

245 Walter Kälin, "Supervising the 1951 Convention Relating to the Status of Refugees: Article 35 and Beyond", in *Refugee Protection in International Law: UNHCR's Global Consultations on International Protection*, ed. Volker Türk, Erica Feller, and Frances Nicholson (Cambridge University Press, 2003), 627.

(2021–2025). It focuses on vulnerable people in the context of migration and asylum in Europe, through supporting and consulting the CoE member states on these issues. In principle, the action plan refers to all vulnerable people in a migratory situation, but it draws particular attention to gender equality and the rights of migrant children. It does not indicate any needs of older migrants.[246]

Contrary to international law, the above -mentioned Directive 2013/33/EU of the European Parliament and of the Council of 26 June 2013, which sets out standards for receiving applicants for international protection and is one of the principal documents constituting the Common European Asylum System, does list older persons as one of the vulnerable groups and obliges the Member States to take into account their specific situation. According to Article 22, the Member States have to assess whether the applicant has special needs and indicate the nature of such needs. In addition, these applicants should receive the necessary healthcare, which includes at least emergency care and the essential treatment of illnesses and severe mental disorders, and states must take into account their particular needs.

In the context of the mass influx of Ukrainians due to the Russian invasion, it is worth noting that Temporary Protection Directive 2001/55/EC,[247] applied in 2022 to war refugees from Ukraine, does not explicitly refer to older persons. They are not mentioned among the categories of people with special needs. According to the directive, Member States should provide necessary medical or other assistance to people such as unaccompanied minors or people who have undergone torture, rape or other serious forms

246 Council of Europe, "Action Plan on Protecting Vulnerable Persons in the Context of Migration and Asylum in Europe (2021–2025)", 2021, https://edoc.coe.int/en/refugees/10241-council-of-europe-action-plan-on-protecting-vulnerable-persons-in-the-context-of-migration-and-asylum-in-europe-2021-2025.html.

247 European Union, "Council Directive 2001/55/EC of 20 July 2001 on Minimum Standards for Giving Temporary Protection in the Event of a Mass Influx of Displaced Persons and on Measures Promoting a Balance of Efforts between Member States in Receiving Such Persons and Bearing the Consequences Thereof" (O. J. L 212, 07.08.2001, pp. 12–23, 2001), https://eur-lex.europa.eu/eli/dir/2001/55/oj.

of psychological, physical or sexual violence. The phrase "such as" makes it possible to assume that states also have obligations towards older people with specific needs, but the lack of an explicit indication means the host state's authorities assisting displaced persons may overlook a specific situation of a person arising from the overlapping torture suffered and old age.

The Common European Asylum System, of which the aforementioned directives form a part, has proved ineffective during the migration crisis and the constant migratory pressure on European countries, especially those on the EU's external borders. Therefore, the New Pact on Migration and Asylum was proposed in 2020 and agreed between the European Parliament and the Council in December 2023.[248] It will be operational from summer 2026.[249]

---

248 See the Statement by President von der Leyen on the political agreement on the Pact on Migration and Asylum, https://ec.europa.eu/commission/presscorner/detail/en/STATEMENT_23_6781.
Brussels, 20 December 2023

249 Regulation (EU) 2024/1356 of the European Parliament and of the Council of 14 May 2024 introducing the screening of third-country nationals at the external borders and amending Regulations (EC) No. 767/2008, (EU) 2017/2226, (EU) 2018/1240 and (EU) 2019/817, O. J. L, 2024/1356, 22.5.2024, https://eur-lex.europa.eu/legal-content/EN/TXT/?uri=CELEX%3A32024R1356; Regulation (EU) 2024/1351 of the European Parliament and of the Council of 14 May 2024 on asylum and migration management, amending Regulations (EU) 2021/1147 and (EU) 2021/1060 and repealing Regulation (EU) No. 604/2013, O. J., 2024/1351, 22.5.2024, https://eur-lex.europa.eu/eli/reg/2024/1351/oj; Regulation (EU) 2024/1348 the European Parliament and of the Council of 14 May 2024 establishing a common procedure for international protection in the Union and repealing Directive 2013/32/EU, O. J. L, 2024/1348, 22.5.2024, ELI: http://data.europa.eu/eli/reg/2024/1348/oj; Regulation (EU) 2024/1349 of the European Parliament and of the Council of 14 May 2024 establishing a return border procedure, and amending Regulation (EU) 2021/1148, OJ L, 2024/1349, 22.5.2024, ELI: http://data.europa.eu/eli/reg/2024/1349/oj; Regulation (EU) 2024/1349 of the European Parliament and of the Council of 14 May 2024 establishing a return border procedure, and amending Regulation (EU) 2021/1148, O. J. L, 2024/1349, 22.5.2024, ELI: http://data.europa.eu/eli/reg/2024/1349/oj; Regulation (EU) 2024/1358 of the European Parliament and of the Council of 14 May 2024 on the establishment of "Eurodac" for the comparison of biometric data in order to effectively apply Regulations (EU) 2024/1351 and (EU) 2024/1350 of the European Parliament and of the Council and Council Directive 2001/55/EC

The New Pact on Migration and Asylum is a set of regulations, directives and policies intending to manage and normalise migration for the long term. It focuses, among other things, on the external aspects of migration and asylum policy, primarily in combating irregular migration and border management. However, it raises many objections from NGOs,[250] academia[251] and human rights bodies. Border procedures and screening at the EU borders are the most objectionable. The Human Rights Council Special Procedures Mandate Holders, the Special Rapporteur on the human rights of migrants, the Working Group on Arbitrary Detention, the Special Rapporteur on contemporary forms of slavery, including its causes and consequences and the

---

and to identify illegally staying third-country nationals and stateless persons and on requests for the comparison with Eurodac data by Member States' law enforcement authorities and Europol for law enforcement purposes, amending Regulations (EU) 2018/1240 and (EU) 2019/818 of the European Parliament and of the Council and repealing Regulation (EU) No. 603/2013 of the European Parliament and of the Council O. J. L, 2024/1358, 22.5.2024, ELI: http://data.europa.eu/eli/reg/2024/1358/oj; Directive (EU) 2024/1346 of the European Parliament and of the Council of 14 May 2024 laying down standards for the reception of applicants for international protection, O. J. L, 2024/1346, 22.5.2024, ELI: http://data.europa.eu/eli/dir/2024/1346/oj; Regulation (EU) 2024/1347 of the European Parliament and of the Council of 14 May 2024 on standards for the qualification of third-country nationals or stateless persons as beneficiaries of international protection, for a uniform status for refugees or for persons eligible for subsidiary protection and for the content of the protection granted, amending Council Directive 2003/109/EC and repealing Directive 2011/95/EU of the European Parliament and of the Council, O. J. L, 2024/1347, 22.5.2024, ELI: http://data.europa.eu/eli/reg/2024/1347/oj.

Regulation (EU) 2024/1350 of the European Parliament and of the Council of 14 May 2024 establishing a Union Resettlement and Humanitarian Admission Framework, and amending Regulation (EU) 2021/1147, O. J. L, 2024/1350, 22.5.2024, ELI: http://data.europa.eu/eli/reg/2024/1350/oj; Regulation (EU) 2024/1352 of the European Parliament and of the Council of 14 May 2024 amending Regulations (EU) 2019/816 and (EU) 2019/818 for the purpose of introducing the screening of third-country nationals at the external borders, O. J. L, 2024/1352, 22.5.2024, ELI: http://data.europa.eu/eli/reg/2024/1352/oj.

250 See Amnesty International: https://www.amnesty.org/en/latest/news/2023/12/eu-migration-pact-agreement-will-lead-to-a-surge-in-suffering/

251 See the open letter https://admigov.eu/upload/Call_EU_funded_researchers.pdf.

Special Rapporteur on trafficking in persons, especially women and children have all called on the EU to amend the Pact. They stress that mandatory and comprehensive vulnerability checks, particularly at borders, should be carried out on every migrant, with their consent and respecting their human rights. Such vulnerability testing should occur as soon as possible, so that vulnerable people, including older persons, can be quickly identified and referred to the relevant services and protection authorities to ensure adequate protection from expulsion. Finally, they called on EU Member States to ensure appropriate procedural safeguards, including individual and objective risk assessments of a person's circumstances and protection needs in order to prevent irreparable harm and expulsion.[252]

In part, these demands were taken into account in the last straight negotiation of the Pact. From the perspective of this study, it is essential that older persons ("elderly persons") are also explicitly itemised in relation to the vulnerability checks carried out at the borders as part of the screening procedure for irregular migrants and reception conditions. The border services or other authorities can waive some safeguards in certain circumstances. With significant migration pressure, a lack of resources and/or unawareness about the services, such a situation seems likely. Worth noting is that the obligation to check for vulnerability at borders is not explained in the European Union Agency for Asylum "Strategy on Vulnerability" published in November 2023.[253] However, the EUAA notes that, under the proposed reception directive and the directive on asylum procedures, the Member State must conduct an individual assessment of whether the applicant has special reception needs and/or needs special procedural guarantees. "Elderly

252 "Mandates of the Special Rapporteur on the Human Rights of Migrants; the Working Group on Arbitrary Detention; the Special Rapporteur on Contemporary Forms of Slavery, Including Its Causes and Consequences and the Special Rapporteur on Trafficking in Persons, Especially Women and Children, 15 December 2023, Ref.: OL OTH 144/2023", https://spcommreports.ohchr.org/TMResultsBase/DownLoadPublicCommunicationFile?gId=28674.

253 European Union Agency for Asylum., *EUAA Strategy on Vulnerability: A Harmonised Approach to Vulnerability in the Framework of the Common European Asylum System : November 2023*. (LU: Publications Office, 2023), https://data.europa.eu/doi/10.2847/582590.

people" are itemised among the categories of the vulnerable whose situation should be taken into account by Member States when conducting asylum procedures, reception and classifying them as refugees or beneficiaries of subsidiary protection.[254]

When it comes into force, the New Pact on Migration and Asylum will be the leading standard for the treatment of voluntary and involuntary migrants in the EU and will impact third countries. The Pact's instruments invoke the Geneva Convention Relating to Refugee Status and the European Convention on Human Rights. They declare full respect for human dignity and the application of the EU Charter of Fundamental Rights, but these instruments also leave a lot of discretion to the Member States. Thus, it will depend on the awareness and goodwill of the national services whether older migrants and their particular needs are identified, first at the border and then in the course of the asylum procedure. It is therefore not surprising that the EUAA has developed the aforementioned "Guidance on Vulnerability in Asylum and Reception", promoting a needs-based approach to vulnerability.

Like the current CEAS, it will be confronted with the ECHR. ECtHR jurisprudence may play an essential role in defining "vulnerability" at borders, especially as the court's jurisprudence to date takes an open-ended approach to vulnerability.[255] It seems that the premise of "other status" contained in the ECHR anti-discrimination clause can be used in the case of vulnerability of older forced migrants arriving at the EU borders. In a situation where there is no instrument in Europe similar to the Convention Governing the Specific Aspects of Refugee Problems in Africa of 1969,[256] or even to the Cartagena Declaration on Refugees of 1984[257] adopted in

---

254 European Union Agency for Asylum., 8.

255 Mariavittoria Catanzariti, "The Juridification of Vulnerability in the European Legal Culture", *Oñati Socio-Legal Series* 12, No. 6 (1 December 2022): 1402, https://doi.org/10.35295/osls.iisl/0000-0000-0000-1314.

256 Organization of African Unity, *Convention Governing the Specific Aspects of Refugee Problems in Africa, adopted by the Assembly of Heads of State and Government at its Sixth Ordinary Session*, (Addis-Ababa, 10 September 1969), https://www.unhcr.org/media/oau-convention-governing-specific-aspects-refugee-problems-africa-adopted-assembly-heads.

257 *Cartagena Declaration on Refugees, adopted by the Colloquium on the International Protection of Refugees in Central America, Mexico and Panama,*

the Organization of American States forum,[258] the ECtHR jurisprudence will play a unique role in defining "vulnerability at the border" and the "border harms of human displacement" that emerged in migration law doctrine during the 2015/2016 crisis in the context of the repatriation, non-admission and detention at the borders or the detention of Syrians attempting to enter the European Union.[259]

As research into the situation of older people after the Russian attack on Ukraine clearly shows, they usually do not want, are not able or have enough strength to leave their country, and even their place of residence.[260] In international global law, internally displaced persons are not protected by a treaty but by the Guiding Principles on Internal Displacement. The fourth principle proclaims that all the principles are applied to all Internally displaced persons (IDPs) without discrimination of any kind, including age and disability. In addition, certain internally displaced persons, such as older persons, are entitled to protection and assistance required by their condition and to treatment that takes into account their special needs.[261] Thus, the message of "treatment according to needs" seems to meet the idea of an intersectional approach, but it is certainly very general.

Given that Europe has been a peaceful region since the Second World War until now, except for conflicts in the former Yugoslavia, no instrument on IDPs has been adopted along the lines of, for example, the African Union Convention for the Protection and Assistance of Internally Displaced

---

Cartagena de Indias, Colombia (22 November 1984), https://www.unhcr.org/media/cartagena-declaration-refugees-adopted-colloquium-international-protection-refugees-central.

258 These instruments do not refer to "older/aged refugees.

259 Suzan Ilcan, "The Border Harms of Human Displacement: Harsh Landscapes and Human Rights Violations", *Social Sciences* 10, No. 4 (30 March 2021): 123, https://doi.org/10.3390/socsci10040123.

260 Oksana Mikheieva and Irina Kuznetsova, *Internally Displaced and Immobile People in Ukraine between 2014 and 2022: Older Age and Disabilities as Factors of Vulnerability*, vol. 77, Migration Research Series (Geneva: International Organization for Migration, 2023), 6.

261 UN High Commissioner for Refugees (UNHCR), *Guiding Principles on Internal Displacement*, 22 July 1998, ADM 1.1, PRL 12.1, PR00/98/109, available at: https://www.refworld.org/docid/3c3da07f7.html.

Persons in Africa (the "Kampala Convention") of 2009. It is worth noting is that this obliges state-parties to provide special protection for and assistance to internally displaced persons with special needs, including "the elderly, and persons with disabilities or with communicable diseases."[262]

During times of war, internally displaced persons should also be protected by the international humanitarian law of armed conflicts. The terms "age" and "aged persons" appear several times in the Third and Fourth Geneva Conventions of 1949. They proclaim the principle of equality of treatment, but also allow for exceptions on various grounds, including age, state of health and gender. The Fourth Geneva Convention relating to the Protection of Civilian Persons in Time of War contains provisions referring to establishing hospitals, safety zones, and localities to protect vulnerable people, including "aged persons, " from the effects of war. Indeed, Article 17 says: "The Parties to the conflict shall endeavour to conclude local agreements for the removal from besieged or encircled areas, of wounded, sick, infirm, and aged persons, children and maternity cases, and for the passage of ministers of all religions, medical personnel and medical equipment on their way to such areas."[263]

International humanitarian law and human rights law are invoked in the Inter-American Convention on the Protection of the Human Rights of Older Persons. Article 29 obliges states to "adopt all necessary specific measures to ensure the safety and rights of older persons in situations of risk, including situations of armed conflict, humanitarian emergencies, and disasters, in accordance with the norms of international law, particularly international human rights law and international humanitarian law. States Parties shall adopt assistance measures specific to the needs of older persons in preparedness, prevention, reconstruction, and recovery activities associated with emergencies, disasters, and conflict situations. States Parties shall foster the participation of interested older persons in civil protection protocols in the event of natural disasters."[264]

---

262 *African Union Convention for the Protection and Assistance of Internally Displaced Persons in Africa ("Kampala Convention")*, 23 October 2009, https://www.refworld.org/docid/4ae572d82.html.

263 International Committee of the Red Cross (ICRC), *Geneva Convention Relative to the Protection of Civilian Persons in Time of War (Fourth Geneva Convention)*, 12 August 1949, (UNTS, vol. 75, p. 287).

264 *Supra note* 16.

Meanwhile, Article 14 of the African Protocol obliges states to ensure that older persons receive humane treatment, protection and respect at all times, and that they are not left without necessary medical assistance and care.

The CoE Council of Ministers Recommendation 2014(2) on the promotion of human rights of older persons does not refer to older persons on the move in crises. Certainly, the part dedicated to counteracting violence against older persons should be taken into account in a such situation, but the first assessment of the implementation of the recommendation does not provide the states with any good (or bad) practices in this area.[265] Maybe, Ukraine will take part in the next review, but it is not an obligatory procedure.

Thus, in the Council of Europe, soft law on the rights of older persons does not pay particular attention to internationally or internally displaced older people. The treaties adopted by the African Union and the Organization of American States fora protect older persons experiencing situations of armed conflict, humanitarian emergencies and disasters. However, even these treaties do not mention older asylum seekers and refugees escaping persecution.

In turn, the MIPAA calls on states to recognise the needs of older refugees of various cultural backgrounds growing old in new and unfamiliar surroundings, and to ensure these people have physical access to social services.[266] However, much more attention is paid in the MIPAA to older persons in emergencies. It calls upon equal access by older persons to food, shelter, medical care and other services during and after natural disasters and other humanitarian emergencies. The MIPAA encourages states to include older refugees in all aspects of programme planning and implementation, among other things by helping active individuals to be more self-supporting and promoting better community care initiatives for the very old.

---

265 Steering Committee for Human Rights, "Steering Committee for Human Rights, Report on the Implementation of the Committee of Ministers' Recommendation CM/Rec (2014) 2 on the Promotion of Human Rights of Older Persons Adopted by the CDDH at Its 90th Meeting (27–30 November 2018), CDDH(2018)R90 Addendum 07/01/2019".

266 MIPAA, para 56.

5. Proposed interpretative tools

5.1. *Pacta sunt servanda* and good faith principles

In the absence of a global treaty containing the human rights of older persons with particular provisions dedicated to older migrants, especially forced ones, and given the lack of references to older persons in treaties protecting various types of migrants, an attempt should be made to interpret the current obligations of states in a way that would make older migrants visible to state authorities in their migration and integration policies. Academia and various international bodies have developed several concepts that may be helpful in this regard. Certainly, their application depends on the will of the states, because international law is still state-centric, although it is constantly changing and the voices of other actors, including civil society organisations, can be heard on the international scene. For this reason, it is crucial to start with a basic guideline that is a central principle of international law. Human rights of all human beings stipulated in treaties should be respected by the principle of *pacta sunt servanda,* which is central to the international community and demonstrates the values on which international law is based. By binding themselves to treaties, states agree, as per Article 26 of the Vienna Convention on the Law of Treaties (VCLT), that: "every treaty in force is binding upon the parties to it and must be performed by them in good faith."[267]

Certainly, human rights treaties have their specific nature and are not just a "simple" state-state relationship as their purpose is not to accomplish the reciprocal exchange of rights for the contracting states' mutual benefit, but to protect individuals, especially the most vulnerable, for the common good.[268] However, human rights treaties are not exempted from

267 United Nations, "Vienna Convention on the Law of Treaties" 29 May 1969 (UNTS vol. 1155, p. 331, 1969).

268 European Commission on Human Rights, *Austria v. Italy*, Application No. 788/60, (1961); Inter-American Court of Human Rights, Advisory Opinion Oc-2/82 of September 24, 1982. The Effect of Reservations on the Entry into Force of the American Convention on Human Rights (Arts. 74 And 75) Requested By The Inter-American Commission On Human Rights (Inter-American Court of Human Rights 1982), para. 29.

the *pacta sunt servanda* principle and must be observed by all the bodies of a state party.[269] Thus, they should "respect", "protect" and "fulfil" the rights of all older persons "on the move" and those who became old abroad. However, as argued above, older migrants are largely invisible under the human rights core treaties, as well as in treaties dedicated to various types of migrants. Protecting the invisible is one of the most difficult areas of treaty interpretation.[270] In practice, relevant state authorities should be willing to take steps to "discover" and understand older migrants and their needs. The clear obligation to take steps in this area arises from good faith, which is in scholarship understood as a "principle of international law", and a "standard" of states' conduct.[271] Article 31 sec. 1 VCLT stipulates that "A treaty shall be interpreted in good faith in accordance with the ordinary meaning to be given to the terms of the treaty in their context and in the light of its object and purpose."

"Good faith" makes the treaties effective and makes sense of the substantive content – rights and obligations.[272] It follows from the nature of human rights that the interpretation of human rights treaties should go beyond the advantages or disadvantages of states and lead to the protection of the common interest. If a treaty contains the rights of "every human being," "everyone," "each person" and "all persons," it means that the purpose of the treaty was not to leave anyone behind, even if a relevant category of persons is not precisely indicated in a given treaty.

Malgosia Fitzmaurice noted that the nature of human rights treaties requires a *pro homine* interpretation.[273] It means that state authorities

---

269 Mark E. Villiger, *Commentary on the 1969 Vienna Convention on the Law of Treaties* (London: Brill/Nijhof, 2009), 368.

270 Richard Gardiner, *Treaty Interpretation* (Oxford: Oxford University Press, 2015), 165.

271 Marcin Kałduński, *Zasada Dobrej Wiary w Prawie Miedzynarodowym [The Good Faith Principle in International Law]*, Monografie Prawnicze (Warsaw: C.H. Beck, 2017), 118, 248.

272 Martin Scheinin, "Core Rights and Obligations", in *The Oxford Handbook of International Human Rights Law, Edited by Dinah Shelton* (Oxford: Oxford University Press, 2013), 540.

273 Malgosia Fitzmaurice, "Interpretation of Human Rights Treaties", in *The Oxford Handbook of International Human Rights Law, Edited by Dinah Shelton* (Oxford: Oxford University Press, 2013), 754.

should be particularly diligent when deciding on the cases of older migrants. However, this is challenging indeed as they are doubly absent in international treaties.

For this reason, the good faith of states and their organs in performing their obligations arising from international human treaties may be expressed via a human rights-based approach (HRBA) and needs-based approach when applying ageing and migration policies. The HRBA should go hand in hand with the 2030 Agenda's main motto "leave no one behind." The third concept supporting an understanding of older migrants' rights is "ageing mainstreaming." Finally, the intersectionality of discrimination due to age, migration status and other circumstances should be taken into account.

5.2. The conceptual output of international bodies

International bodies as well as the human rights scholarship have worked out some conceptual tools that can be used to respect, protect and fulfil the human rights of older migrants. In the beginning, the human rights-based approach (HRBA) was drawn up by the United Nations Development Group as part of the general guidelines for UN Agencies in 2003, aimed at guiding dialogue with governments and building a culture of human rights, as well as all UN activities following the human rights principles: universality and inalienability; indivisibility; inter-dependence and inter-relatedness; non-discrimination and equality; participation and inclusion; accountability and the rule of law.[274] Over the years, the HRBA has become a tool for interpreting treaties for states and international organisations including the European Union.

The European Commission, in a Commission Staff Working Document on applying the Human Rights Based Approach to international partnerships, explained that HRBA is a methodology that applies above mentioned working principles to human rights for all.[275]

---

274 UNDG, "United Nations Development Group, The Human Rights Based Approach to Development Cooperation Towards a Common Understanding Among UN Agencies", 2003, https://unsdg.un.org/resources/human-rights-based-approach-development-cooperation-towards-common-understanding-among-un.

275 European Commission, "Commission Staff Working Document. Applying the Human Rights Based Approach to International Partnerships An Updated

In general, the HRBA has two aspects. The first is empowering rights-holders (individuals or social groups) to claim and exercise their rights. The second one is strengthening the capacity of duty-bearers (states or non-state actors) who must respect, protect, promote and fulfil the human rights of rights-holders as well as address various challenges, including managing migration or responding to crises. Thus, the HRBA aims to strengthen the capabilities of both duty-bearers and rights-holders towards discourse and implementing rights and obligations, as well as addressing individuals as rights-holders and empowering them to know, claim and enjoy their human rights.[276]

The international human rights framework and its principles lie at the heart of the HRBA. The primary assumption of its conceptual framework is that all programmes of development cooperation, policies and technical assistance should be aimed at fulfilling human rights as laid down in the Universal Declaration of Human Rights and other international human rights instruments. The UNDHR, in its preamble, stipulates that "Whereas recognition of the inherent dignity and of the equal and inalienable rights of all members of the human family is the foundation of freedom, justice and peace in the world." The phrase "inherent dignity and the equal and inalienable rights of all members of the human family" is also present in both Covenants on Human Rights of 1966 and in the International Convention on the Elimination of All Forms of Racial Discrimination of 1965.

The values of dignity, autonomy, liberty and equality, which all have their foundations in the core human rights treaties and the Universal Declaration of Human Rights, are the first side of HRBA. The second are states' duties to respect, protect and fulfil the human rights of every person.[277]

Toolbox for Placing Rights-Holders at the Centre of EU's Neighbourhood, Development and International Cooperation, Brussels, 30.6.2021 SWD(2021) 179 Final", https://international-partnerships.ec.europa.eu/news-and-events/events/human-rights-based-approach-eu-toolbox-placing-rights-holders-centre-international-partnerships-2021-09-16_en.

276 Manfred Nowak, Karolina Januszewski, and Tina Höffstrater, *All Human Rihts for All* (Vienna/Gratz: Insertina, 2012), 277.

277 Bridget Lewis, Kelly Purser, and Kirsty Mackie, *The Human Rights of Older Persons: A Human Rights-Based Approach to Elder Law* (Springer, Singapore, 2020), 67–81.

Despite a fairly ambiguous, controversial and complex character and various interpretative problems,[278] human dignity is constantly invoked on international forums and recognised as the basis for human rights and gap-filling in their interpretation.[279] Its function is to protect those most vulnerable,[280] including those excluded or at risk of exclusion, such as older migrants, asylum seekers, refugees, war refugees and displaced persons. It

278 Henk Botha, "Human Dignity in Comparative Perspective", *Stellenbosch Law Review* 20, No. 2 (2009): 171–220, http://hdl.handle.net/10019.1/103998; Catherine Dupré, *The Age of Dignity: Human Rights and Constitutionalism in Europe*. (Oxford ; Portland, Oregon: Hart Publishing, 2015); Christian Erk, *Health, Rights and Dignity : Philosophical Reflections on an Alleged Human Right* (Paris, Frankfurt, Lancaster, New Brunswick: Ontos Verlag, 2011); Jürgen Habermas, "The Concept of Human Dignity and the Realistic Utopia of Human Rights", *Methaphilosophy* 41, No. 4 (2010): 464–80; Michael Karlberg, "Reframing Human Dignity", in *Interdisciplinary Perspectives on Human Dignity and Human Rights*, Hoda Mahmoudi Michael L. Penn (Bingley: Emerald Publishing Limited, 2020), 35–48, doi.org/10.1108/978-1-78973-821-620191004; Hoda Mahmoudi, "Universal Consciousness of Human Dignity", in *Interdisciplinary Perspectives on Human Dignity and Human Rights,* Hoda Mahmoudi, Michael L. Penn (Bingley: Emerald Publishing Limited, 2020), 17–26, 10.1108/978-1-78973-821-620191002; Christopher McCrudden, "Human Dignity and Judicial Interpretation of Human Rights", *European Journal of International Law* 19, No. 4 (2008): 655–724, http://www.ejil.org/pdfs/19/4/1658.pdf; Eduard Picker, *Godność człowieka a życie ludzkie* (Warszawa: Oficyna Naukowa, 2007); Michael Rosen, *Dignity. Its History and Meaning* (Cambridge Massachusetts and London: Harvard University Press, 2012).

279 Glenn Hughes, "The Concept of Dignity in the Universal Declaration of Human Rights", *The Journal of Religious Ethics* 39, No. 1 (2011): 1–24, http://www.jstor.org/stable/23020122; M Glen Johnson and Janusz Symonides, *The Universal Declaration of Human Rights A History of Its Creation and Implementation 1948–1998* (Paris: UNESCO Publishing, 1998). Pinghua Sun, "P. C. Chang's Concept of Human Dignity for the Universal Declaration of Human Rights", *Journal of East Asia & International Law.* 12, No. 1 (2019), http://journal.yiil.org/home/pdf/publications/2019_12_1_pdf/jeail_v12n1_05.pdf; Shultziner and Guy E. Carmi, "Human Dignity in National Constitutions: Functions, Promises and Danger", *The American Journal of Comparative Law* 62, No. 2 (2014): 461–90, https://www.researchgate.net/publication/259979648.

280 Shultziner and Carmi, "Human Dignity in National Constitutions: Functions, Promises and Danger", 479.

appears as an essential value shared globally by the international community, regardless of cultural traditions and the legal system.[281]

Dignity is a reference point for equity, as human beings are "free and equal."[282] Equity refers to how fairly services, opportunities and access are distributed across groups of people or places.[283] Equal access to healthcare services, education, new technologies, culture, etc. is crucial for older migrants to participate in the life of hosting society. In the case of older persons, and particularly older non-citizens, equality requires solidarity, which also arises from the inherent dignity of all human beings and "connects a concern for the well-being of the other with the universality of human rights and the protection of dignity."[284] Finally, dignity is also interpreted as respect or the right to respect and the right to respectful treatment.[285] The prevalent phenomena of ageism and racism are particular threats to human dignity.

That is why, in the case of older migrants, even if there is no hard international norm on states' obligations toward various types of older migrants, the HRBA requires that states and their organs show goodwill and adopt a positive attitude to consider each migrant's case from the perspective of their human rights and dignity.

Justice Mensah, Amos Mensah and Aba Mensah Nyameyie indicate that people being left behind are often economically, socially, spatially and/or politically excluded for various reasons, including due to their age. They lack the choices and capabilities that enable them to benefit from human development; they are disconnected from societal institutions and lack information networks and economic and social support systems. They are

---

281 Mahmoudi, "Universal Consciousness of Human Dignity", 21.

282 Rosen, *Dignity. Its History and Meaning*, 38.

283 Magdalena Małecka – Łyszczek and Radosław Mędrzycki, "Axiological Paradigm of Social Inclusion Intensification – Selected Remarks", *Review of European and Comparative Law* XXXVIII (2019): 86, https://doi.org/10.31743/recl.4826.

284 Ruud ter Muelen, "Solidarity, Justice, and Recognition of the Other", *Theoretical Medicine and Bioethics,* 37, No. 6 (2016): 525, https://doi.org/10.1007/s11017-016-9387-3.

285 Erk, *Health, Rights and Dignity : Philosophical Reflections on an Alleged Human Right*, 230; Rosen, *Dignity. Its History and Meaning*, 54.

invisible when policies and programmes are being developed and have no voice to affect them. Moreover, a new generation of inequalities and discrimination is opening up around education and technology.[286] It appears that older migrants are the most unlisted-to of all vulnerable groups and older migrants are the most unheard of all vulnerable groups and the most left behind. By their migration status, they no longer belong to "their" society, but also to the host society. They are also not heard and are left behind because of the (often multiple) stereotypes, prejudices, and age discrimination that constitute ageism.

That is why the well-known concept from the 2030 Agenda for Sustainable Development – "leave no one behind" (LNOB) can be applied in the interpretation of states' obligations towards older migrants. The agenda's political declaration recognises the "positive contribution of migrants for inclusive growth" and the "multi-dimensional reality" of migration. Migration issues are present in several goals and targets, especially in Goal 10 on reducing inequalities, calling states on "facilitating orderly, safe, regular and responsible migration and mobility of people" as well as the implementation of planned and well-managed migration policies (target 10.7). Another target crucial for older migrant workers is reducing the costs of transferring remittances (target 10.c). Moreover, the situation of migrant workers is addressed in the goal on decent work and economic development. Migration also coincides with targets on sustainable cities and resilience in the face of climate change.[287]

On the other hand, the 2030 Agenda does not refer explicitly to older persons, but at least gives space for further developments as it promotes the

---

286 Justice Mensah, Amos Mensah, and Aba Mensah Nyameyie, "Understanding and Promoting the 'Leaving No One behind' Ambition Regarding the Sustainable Development Agenda: A Review", *Visegrad Journal on Bioeconomy and Sustainable Development* 11, No. 1 (2022): 8, https://doi.org/0.2478/vjbsd-2022-0002.

287 UN General Assembly, "Transforming Our World: The 2030 Agenda for Sustainable Development, Resolution Adopted by the General Assembly on 25 September 2015, A/RES/70/1", 2015, https://www.unfpa.org/resources/transforming-our-world-2030-agenda-sustainable-development.

inclusion of people of all ages.[288] Certainly, older migrants are not indicated in any way in the agenda's targets.

In order to not leave older migrants behind, one can therefore rely on guidelines of a general nature provided by the UN bodies and doctrinal interpretation. For example, some guidelines may be sought in the post-2030 Agenda developments, including the mentioned UNDESA report of 2016. It explains that "ensuring that no one is left behind' encompasses multiple meanings. For some, it will mean focusing action on disadvantaged groups of society, for example, people living in poverty, women, indigenous people, youth, older people, persons with disabilities, migrants, or people in conflict and post-conflicts situations ..."[289]

The United Nations Development Programme (UNDP) proposes three level actions to make the motto "leave no one behind " real. First, governments must examine why people are left behind, which involves collecting and use more and better-disaggregated data and people-driven information. The second step is enabling excluded people to participate in decision-making processes and establish safe and inclusive mechanisms for their civic engagement. Finally, states should enact policies, laws, reforms, and interventions to confront the factors that leave people behind across SDGs. It means that all stakeholders, duty bearers and rights holders will have to shape, implement and improve policies to reduce inequality and maintain minimum welfare standards.[290] Thus, collecting data and information on the age of migrants and their needs could be an example of the first stem. The second one could be applicable mainly concerning integration

---

288 Patricia Conboy, "Older-Age Exclusion and the 2030 Agenda for Sustainable Development", in *Social Exclusion in Later Life Interdisciplinary and Policy Perspectives*, Kieran Walsh, Thomas Scharf, Sofie Van Regenmortel, Anna Wanka, International Perspectives on Aging (359–372: Springer Nature, 2021), 359, 030-51406-8 (eBook) https://doi.org/10.1007/978-3-030-51406-8.

289 UNDESA, "Leaving No One behind: The Imperative of Inclusive Development Report on the World Social Situation 2016" (United Nations, 2016), 4, https://www.un.org/esa/socdev/rwss/2016/full-report.pdf.

290 UNDP, "United Nations Development Programme What Does It Mean to Leave No One behind? A UNDP Discussion Paper and Framework for Implementation July 2018", 2018, 4–5, https://www.undp.org/publications/what-does-it-mean-leave-no-one-behind.

policy. The last level requires cooperation with civil society organisations, which usually know the situation of vulnerable migrants.

In general, LNOB is an ambitious concept, but very generic, and its efficiency is difficult to measure. Moreover, today it is difficult to imagine this LNOB model being applied in practice to undocumented migrants.

Another concept worked out at the international level that can help in the recognition of older migrants' needs and rights is "mainstreaming ageing." It is a concept that has been promoted since the 1990s, particularly in connection with the International Year of Older Persons in 1999. Its main message was "towards society for all ages,"[291] and is continuing under the Madrid process of "building a society for all ages." The idea of a society for all ages directly corresponds with the 2030 Agenda's concept of "leaving no one behind."

"Mainstreaming ageing" is a dynamic and developing concept. In 2021, under the auspices of the United Nations Economic Commission for Europe, new "Guidelines for Mainstreaming Ageing" were drawn up[292] to support governments in building a strategic framework for mainstreaming ageing. They are not dedicated to any specific age group, e.g. older migrants. However, they consider ageing from a societal perspective and an individual life course perspective, taking into consideration the changing needs and capacities of human beings and proposing a coherent, holistic policy towards all generations (from the cradle to the grave).

The guidelines describe "mainstreaming ageing," as a strategy, process and multi-dimensional effort of integrating ageing issues into all policy fields and levels. The ultimate objective is to achieve a more equitable societal development that will benefit all social and age groups. The most important

291 UN General Assembly, "Resolution of 16 October 1992, 2 Proclamation on Ageing, A/RES/47/5", https://www.un.org/development/desa/ageing/resources/international-year-of-older-persons-1999/resolution-475.html; UN General Assembly, "Conceptual Framework of a Programme for the Preparation and Observance of the International Year of Older Persons in 1999 : Report of the Secretary-General, A/50/114 22 March 1995", https://digitallibrary.un.org/record/177179.

292 UNECE, "Guidelines for Mainstreaming Ageing" (Geneva: United Nations Economic Commission for Europe, 2021), https://unece.org/sites/default/files/2021-03/ECE-WG.1-37_Guidelines_for-Mainstreaming_Ageing_1.pdf.

is that "the mainstreaming ageing" approach considers heterogeneity and diversity within and across age groups and promotes intra- and intergenerational solidarity and social cohesion.

The mainstreaming ageing approach is also present in the European forum. In March 2021, the EU Council adopted Conclusions on Mainstreaming Ageing in Public Policies aiming to face long-term socio-economic and demographic implications of ageing to encourage the EU to take action enabling older people to enjoy their fundamental rights and reach their full potential. Most importantly, from the perspective of this study, is that the council encourages states to develop a constructive culture towards the diverse groups of older people, fostering a positive image of them, keeping in mind their heterogeneous needs, opportunities and preferences, to promote an inclusive society that does not segregate, discriminate or spread prejudice against older people.[293]

However, concerning older migrants, greater hopes can be placed on the Rome Declaration of the Ministerial Conference on Ageing, adopted in 2022 in which the representatives of states declared the introduction of mainstreaming ageing in all policies at all levels of government to create a society for all ages by developing or strengthening, as well as coordinating, national strategic policies. Their actions are to include, among other things:

- intensifying age- and gender-sensitive research and data collection disaggregated by gender, age and disability and the diverse situation of older people to inform evidence-based policy, monitoring and evaluation;
- building a human rights-based, lifespan-oriented approach to mainstreaming ageing;
- addressing multiple and intersecting forms of discrimination and the diverse needs, preferences and capacities of older people;
- addressing the challenges posed by emergencies (including COVID-19) and conflicts and strengthening international cooperation in this area.[294]

293 Council of the European Union, "Council Conclusions on Mainstreaming Ageing in Public Policies, Outcome of Proceedings, General Secretariat of the Council to Delegations, Brussels, 12 March 2021 6976/21, SOC 142", 2021, https://data.consilium.europa.eu/doc/document/ST-6976-2021-INIT/en/pdf.

294 UNECE, "Rome Ministerial Declaration "A Sustainable World for All Ages: Joining Forces for Solidarity and Equal Opportunities Throughout Life"

The declaration covers a range of ideas about solidarity, the "no one left behind" concept and a human rights-based approach. It can be presumed that, by declaring the implementation of "mainstreaming ageing" into all policies, state delegations also considered migration, asylum and war refugee policies. On the other hand, the Rome Declaration is merely a declaration with no legally binding force, the non-implementation of which has no legal consequences.

Due to the adoption of the New Pact on Migration and Asylum, the concept of the needs-based approach promoted by the EUAA should also be highlighted, as the new instruments comprising the entire asylum system legal instruments leave states a considerable degree of discretion in the identification of applicants in a vulnerable situation and how to assess and respond to their needs. This means that the standard of identifying the needs of older migrants can vary from one EU country to another. Thus, individual-based approaches aim to develop a customised response that considers the applicant's specific situation. Adequate response strategies can help immigration services identify tailored special reception conditions and special procedural guarantees for vulnerable people, including older asylum seekers.

The mentioned needs-based approach consists of four response strategies – intensification, prioritisation, differentiation and specialisation, which follow identifying vulnerabilities and assessing individual needs. Here, a prerequisite for the identification of asylum seekers' special needs is listening to them. In some cases it means providing them with a social assistant or enabling contact with NGOs.

According to the EUAA, intensification means allocating more resources to support applicants with special needs adequately. Prioritisation requires enabling faster access to necessary services for applicants with special needs, as waiting may aggravate their vulnerable situation. Differentiation is based on the availability of distinct yet equivalent options for reception conditions, related services, and procedural guarantees. Finally, specialisation means

---

MIPPA 20, 16–17 June 2022", paras. 40–45. https://unece.org/sites/default/files/2022-06/Rome__Ministerial_Declaration.pdf.

providing applicants with internal or external services with distinct knowledge and competencies to respond to their needs.[295]

According to the EUAA, when implementing strategies to identify asylum seekers' vulnerability, the relevant stakeholders should follow the principles of confidentiality, data protection, do no harm, accountability, respect for diversity, integrity, and, certainly, fundamental rights.[296]

If all of the above-mentioned concepts are to help interpret states' obligations towards safeguarding the human rights of older migrants, they should be accompanied by an intersectional approach, based on an understanding of the overlapping barriers to the enjoyment of these rights and the reasons for their exclusion. The intersectional approach to older migrants relies on understanding the essence of the human rights of migrants and, at the same time, older people, and helps make the idea of the interdependence of civil and political rights and economic, social and cultural rights real.[297] It is a *sine qua non* condition for recognising and then meeting the diverse and overlapping needs of older migrants of various categories. Thus, it can give substance to the Agenda 2030 message, "leave no one behind."[298] Indeed, promoting such an approach in international forums and documents, including the future Convention on the Rights of Older Persons, does not guarantee that states will take into account the needs of older migrants, especially since migration matters are closely linked to security issues. However, it at least offers a chance to avoid or reduce the exclusion of older migrants based on their migration situation and age.

---

295 European Union Agency for Asylum (2024), pp. 23 – 24.

296 European Union Agency for Asylum (2024),p.16.

297 Gerard Quinn, "Reflections on the Value of Intersectionality to the Development of Non-Discrimination Law," *The Equal Rights Review* Sixteen (2016), 72. https://www.equalrightstrust.org/equal-rights-review-volume-sixteen-2016.

298 UN General Assembly, *Transforming Our World: The 2030 Agenda for Sustainable Development, Resolution Adopted by the General Assembly on 25 September 2015*, A/RES/70/1, https://www.unfpa.org/resources/transforming-our-world-2030-agenda-sustainable-development.

Final remarks

The above overview of international and European law that directly, or more often indirectly, affects older migrants has its limitations. In its framework, only a portion of the provisions have been identified and, of course, they are not a response to all the vulnerabilities of older migrants. For example, the issue of family reunification deserves a separate analysis. International jurisprudence was only briefly mentioned in this study, and yet it represents research material that can be explored endlessly. However, this limited study, which is part of more extensive research on including older persons from an international law perspective, allows for several remarks.

1. It may be argued that the lack of any binding treaty provisions causes the ambiguity of states' obligations on older persons' rights, including the rights of those most "left behind." These obligations are imperceptible at first glance. Moreover, under the existing normative framework, states have many possibilities to avoid or soften their duties in the area of human rights. States are free to bind themselves to treaties and often opt out of those that impose obligations on migration. They often make reservations about treaties and, if they can choose "à la carte" obligations, they ignore those provisions of crucial importance for older migrants. Finally, they enjoy a considerable margin of appreciation in implementing their obligations. For this reason, adopting a Convention on the Rights of the Older Persons indicating the obligations of states towards voluntary and involuntary migrants is highly desirable. Thus, the first and fundamental condition for the inclusion of older migrants in international discourse, which may perhaps translate into action by states on domestic grounds, is their explicit identification in treaty law.
2. General human rights law, usually adopted decades ago, often fails to address the specific rights of older persons and the multifaceted and intersectional discrimination based on age and migration status. The same observation applies to humanitarian law of armed conflict, which should at least partly respond to older displaced people's vulnerability. On the other hand, however, regardless of when the norms in question were adopted, international law requires states to maintain a "standard of good faith" when implementing their obligations. This means that governments, when formulating their migration and integration

policies and making specific decisions, should operate through the lens of ageing mainstreaming, a human rights-based and needs-based approaches, and the concept of "leaving no one behind." It is also essential for governments to understand the intersectionality of older people's vulnerabilities, as well as the intersectionality of the discrimination they experience. Moreover, the vulnerabilities of various types of migrants need a case-by-case study to recognise migrants' needs. Moreover, an awareness of older migrants' vulnerabilities and their specific needs will allow for an understanding of the barriers to their enjoyment of human rights, and for states to take steps towards them that will at least reduce these barriers.

3. International human rights bodies are responsible for reminding states of their obligations. The courting of older migrants by Human Rights Council Special Procedures Mandate Holders and human rights treaty bodies is another element in strengthening the visibility of older migrants. It is also logical that if states are sensitised to older migrants' vulnerabilities through these procedures, they will bring them to the attention of other states through the UPR process.
4. The above review has also shown that both hard and soft international law on older persons, on the one hand, and migration, on the other, make little reference to older migrants and their specific situations. There are groups of older migrants, such as older asylum seekers or undocumented migrant workers, who are usually not visible in international hard and soft law documents. Hard international law on various types of migrants has come to a standstill. For example, international law has consistently failed to answer the question of how to protect climate migrants effectively. There is an apparent gap in contemporary international law regarding the granting of protection to what are known as climate migrants or refugees[299] and internally displaced persons.[300] Meanwhile, the status of refugees is still governed by the 1951

---

299 Both notions are used in the scholarship and in the international reports. See International Organization for Migration, *Glossary on Migration*.

300 Giovanni Sciaccaluga, "Why States Should Protect Forced Climate Migrants", in *International Law and the Protection of "Climate Refugees"*, by Giovanni Sciaccaluga (Cham: Springer International Publishing, 2020), 127, Jesús Verdú Baeza, "Climate Refugees, Human Rights and the Principle of

convention. The Convention on the Protection of Migrant Workers dates back more than 30 years and is not particularly popular among host countries. Internally displaced persons have not received protection under a universal treaty at all. Without legal solutions and given their outdated form, it is challenging to expect specific solutions for vulnerable migrants. Moreover, the last several years have shown that a hitherto relatively peaceful Europe has yet to need comprehensive provisions for the most vulnerable, including older people, in times of crisis, such as wars or mass violations of human rights. Given Europe's demographic structure, migratory movements and political situation, it may be necessary to adopt new legal solutions at a supranational level. Furthermore, given the development of international law towards the protection of the rights of older persons and in the face of global ageing, both general migration law and European law, therefore, need to be refreshed by, among other things, taking into account the specific nature of migration in older age and emigration ageing.

5. In the discussed area, a unique role is played not only by human rights procedures but also by various guidelines and reports of international bodies that highlight the problems of older migrants, especially those who are involuntary, and point to actions that should be taken by international bodies, governments and other stakeholders to ensure that older people in a migratory situation face as few barriers as possible to the exercise of their human rights. Worth noting are also reports drawn up by international bodies and NGOs advocating for migrants' and older persons' human rights.[301]

   However, it will be up to governments managing migration to take advantage of the guidance in these documents. After all, the situation of migrants, particularly voluntary migrants, is mainly regulated by national laws. Therefore, some expectations can be placed in the educational role

---

Non-Refoulement", *Paix et Securite Internationales*, No. 11 (2023), https://doi.org/10.25267/Paix_secur_int.2023.i11.1401.

301 UN OHCHR and Global Migration Group, *Principles and Practical Guidance on the Protection of the Human Rights of Migrants in Vulnerable Situations. Report of the United Nations High Commissioner for Human Rights, 3 January 2018, A/HRC/37/34*; UNHCR and HelpAge International, "A Claim to Dignity: Ageing on the Move. Regional Assessment on the Situation and Needs of Older Persons on the Move in the Americas" (Geneva, 2021), https://www.unhcr.org/media/claim-dignity-ageing-move.

of international human rights law and its mechanisms in explaining to states their obligations based on the concepts of a human rights-based approach, leaving no one behind and ageing mainstreaming.

Annexe

A. Global forum

UNHCR's Policy on Older Refugees

as endorsed at the 17th Meeting of the Standing Committee, 29 February – 2 March 2000

I. Preliminary observations

1. Older refugees make up a larger proportion of the UNHCR caseload than may be generally recognised. It is commonly assumed that older people are more likely to choose to stay in their place of origin, or, more tragically still, to perish in flight or to pine away and die in exile. In fact, older refugees make up some 8.5 % of the overall population of concern to UNHCR, and reach up to more than 30 % for some caseloads. The majority of these older persons are women. The definition of an older person adopted by the World Health Organization is a person over 60 years old. However, the application of this policy will respect factors such as life expectancy and cultural norms that differ from region to region.
2. While the plight of older refugees can be severe, they should not be seen only as passive, dependent recipients of assistance. This policy seeks to highlight that older refugees often serve as formal and informal leaders of communities; they are valuable resources for guidance and advice, and transmitters of culture, skills and crafts that are important in preserving the traditions of the dispossessed and displaced. Older refugees can and do make an active contribution to the well-being of their next-of-kin, and only become totally dependent in the final stages of frailty, disability and illness. Older persons have taken the lead in return to countries as far afield as Croatia and Liberia. Older persons can also contribute to peace and reconciliation measures. Good programming requires that these roles are utilised. Alongside these positive aspects, however, are a number of needs that characterise the situation of older refugees.

II. The challenges

3. Three major problems facing most refugees, in particular older refugees, are: social disintegration, negative social selection and chronic dependency. In the case of the older refugees these problems are often compounded.
4. Social disintegration occurs as the formal or informal social support systems erode in periods of economic decline or when war, flight, economic or security pressures cause the separation and dispersal of families. In either case, the number of elderly persons in need, and who are left to their own resources, increases. In many cases, families have had to make painful choices about abandonment in order to survive. In Eastern Europe, the comprehensive pension, health care and social welfare systems have not survived the transition to a market economy, which has led to a dramatic drop in the standard of living of all those who had to depend on welfare provided by the State, most especially the old. Elderly internally displaced and returnees have been particularly affected. Hardest hit are the victims of forced displacement who have lost not only their former entitlements but also their homes and other economic assets. A further aggravating factor has been the erosion of traditional support networks. Economic decline, social mobility and the pace of social change have eroded community values, so that the old, in particular older refugees, may no longer enjoy the same authority, care and attention that they had in the past. In addition, the scourges of HIV/AIDS and war have often wiped out an entire middle generation, thereby contributing further to the disintegration of the social fabric; invariably, it is the older refugee who is called upon to assume more immediate responsibility towards the younger members of the family.
5. Negative social selection occurs when refugee camps and collective centres empty over time, with those who are young, healthy and able-bodied the first to depart, leaving behind the weaker and more vulnerable members of the group, namely the sick, the handicapped, single mothers with young children and the elderly. When resources are limited, these groups are particularly vulnerable. The plight of the elderly is particularly tragic. Often they have nowhere to go and no one to take care of them. In this way, some collective centres in Central and Eastern Europe have become geriatric wards in all but name.

6. This residual caseload of solitary older persons, unable to secure State benefits or family support, may become dependent on UNHCR for long periods of time. Here UNHCR faces a particular challenge. It must work to ensure that their experience of exile is not compounded by poverty and destitution, while seeking to avoid chronic dependency by helping them regularize their status and obtain access to all possible benefits, entitlements and rights. This is not an easy task where dramatic social and economic change in asylum countries has caused a marked decline in the living standards of all residents.
7. A comprehensive policy on elderly refugees must take into account both these needs and the contribution they are able to make, commensurate with their age and status.

III. An integrated approach

8. UNHCR's management of refugee protection and assistance programmes requires that its staff and those of implementing partners recognise the different needs and potential of all refugees, be they young or old. Their needs are not well served when, particularly in emergencies, refugees are treated as an undifferentiated mass of humanity. To ensure that UNHCR's programmes become more sensitive to the needs and potential contribution of older refugees, a specific policy on older refugees is needed.
9. Older people's needs must not, however, be addressed in isolation. They are met normally and most effectively within the context of family and community of which they are a part. Consequently, UNHCR needs to strengthen the capacity of families and communities to meet their own needs and incorporate older people within them. Thus this policy should be seen as linked to the High Commissioner's Policy on Refugee Women and the Policy on Refugee Children. Efforts to mainstream the policy priorities relating to refugee women, children and adolescents, need to be extended to the elderly.
10. Older people of concern need to be integrated within UNHCR's overall protection and assistance programming process. Although often at a disadvantage through reduced physical capability, older persons are a valuable resource with much to offer. The potential contributions of older persons must not be overlooked. They are people with a wealth of accumulated experience and knowledge, well able to participate in

decisions and activities that affect their own lives and those of their families and communities. Efforts on behalf of older refugees that see them only as vulnerable individuals to be fed and sheltered are not sufficient; they must be treated as contributing members of their communities.

IV. Organizational goal

11. UNHCR's primary goal in relation to older refugees is that:

Older male and female refugees, and other older persons of concern to the Office, live their later years in dignity and security, contributing actively to their families and communities for as long as it remains possible for them to do so, and are offered care and support if they become physically or mentally frail.

V. General principles

In formulating this Policy, UNHCR re-affirms its support for the United Nations Principles for Older Persons, based on the International Plan of Action on Ageing.[1]

VI. Objectives

13. On the basis of these Principles, UNHCR staff, and those of its implementing partners, should endeavour to address the protection and assistance needs of older persons of concern to UNHCR in a gender-sensitive manner and ensure their equality of access to all measures that will promote their participation and well-being. To this end, UNHCR staff will pursue the following specific objectives:

(i) Early identification of, and care for, older persons with special needs in an emergency;
(ii) The protection of older persons at risk from neglect and abandonment;
(iii) The regularization of the status of older persons so that they can receive benefits to which they are entitled;

(iv) The consistent incorporation, from the beginning of a refugee situation, of gender and age-sensitive protection and assistance criteria that will thus be useful for assessing, monitoring and addressing the needs and vulnerabilities of older persons;

(v) The improvement of the efficiency and effectiveness of protection and assistance programmes by ensuring that adequate attention is given to the needs and resources of all members of the population in a way that takes into account specific needs deriving from gender;

(vi) The improvement of data collection and needs assessment in order to have a more accurate picture of the refugee population and hence more effective targeting of programmes for specific age and social groups;

(vii) In all phases of programme planning and implementation, the role and potential contribution of older refugees should be borne in mind; in this way, they will have the means and opportunities, wherever possible, to continue to realize their potential; such an approach would also promote better community care initiatives for the very old;

(viii) A strengthened community services input in UNHCR programmes to ensure effective outreach to all refugees, and a holistic approach which sees older refugees as part of family and community;

(ix) Responsible phasing-out of UNHCR care for older persons of concern, through the establishment of programmes by local NGOs, relevant Government Ministries (not solely the Ministry responsible for refugee affairs) or in conjunction with international development agencies. Such phasing-out must include a component of capacity-building of national and local structures, where necessary;

(x) The training of UNHCR and implementing partner staff based on more in-depth study of the different needs related to the gender of the elderly population, so as to understand and address appropriately, within their areas of competence, the specific needs of older persons;

(xi) The promotion of awareness of, and response to, the particular needs of older refugees through information strategies directed at the Governments of both countries of asylum and countries of origin, donors, NGOs, other United Nations bodies and the public at large.

VII. Conclusion

14. Older refugees will always have special needs, but the High Commissioner does not call for addressing the needs of older refugees separate from those of other refugees. Indeed UNHCR's Policy on Older Refugees has been formulated with the hope that future efforts on behalf of older persons will have become so well integrated into all aspects of protection and programme planning and implementation that a separate Policy on Older Refugees will cease, in time, to be necessary. Commitment to, and due regard for, the components of a policy aimed at older refugees are pre-requisites for ensuring their participation and well-being. Much of what remains to be done for older refugees, therefore, can be accomplished with the resources normally provided by host governments and the international community.

Madrid International Plan of Action on Ageing
Second World Assembly on Ageing, Madrid, 8–12 April 2002

Excerpts

Issue 3: Rural development, migration and urbanization

[...]

30. Despite restrictions on legal international migration, migration flows have increased internationally. In developing countries and countries with economies in transition, economic support, including remittances from children abroad, is often a vital lifeline to older persons and through them to their communities and local economies. As international migrants from earlier decades grow older, some Governments are seeking to assist older migrants.

[...]

34. **Objective 3: Integration of older migrants within their new communities.**

Actions

(a) Encourage supportive social networks for older migrants;
(b) Design measures to assist older migrants to sustain economic and health security;
(c) Develop community-based measures to prevent or offset the negative consequences of urbanization, such as the establishment of centres for older persons;
(d) Encourage housing design to promote intergenerational living, where culturally appropriate and individually desired;
(e) Assist families to share accommodation with older family members who desire it;
(f) Develop policies and programmes that facilitate, as appropriate, and as consistent with national laws, the integration of older migrants into the social, cultural, political and economic life of countries of destination and encourage respect for those migrants;
(g) Remove linguistic and cultural barriers when providing public services to older migrants

[…]

Issue 8: Emergency situations

54. In emergency situations, such as natural disasters and other humanitarian emergencies, older persons are especially vulnerable and should be identified as such because they may be isolated from family and friends and less able to find food and shelter. They may also be called upon to assume primary caregiving roles. Governments and humanitarian relief agencies should recognise that older persons can make a positive contribution in coping with emergencies in promoting rehabilitation and reconstruction.
55. **Objective 1: Equal access by persons to food, shelter and medical care and other services during and after natural disasters and other humanitarian emergencies.**

Actions

(a) Take concrete measures to protect and assist older persons in situations of armed conflict and foreign occupation, including through the provision of physical and mental rehabilitation services for those who are disabled in these situations;
(b) Call upon Governments to protect, assist and provide humanitarian assistance and humanitarian emergency assistance to older persons in situations of internal displacement in accordance with General Assembly resolutions;
(c) Locate and identify older persons in emergency situations and ensure inclusion of their contributions and vulnerabilities in needs assessment reports;
(d) Raise awareness among relief agency personnel of the physical and health issues specific to older persons and of ways to adapt basic needs support to their requirements;
(e) Aim to ensure that appropriate services are available, that older persons have physical access to them and that they are involved in planning and delivering services as appropriate;
(f) Recognise that older refugees of different cultural backgrounds growing old in new and unfamiliar surroundings are often in special need of social networks and of extra support and aim to ensure that they have physical access to such services;
(g) Make explicit reference to, and design national guidelines for, assisting older persons in disaster relief plans, including disaster preparedness, training for relief workers and availability of services and goods;
(h) Assist older persons to re-establish family and social ties and address their post-traumatic stress;
(i) Following disasters, put in place mechanisms to prevent the targeting and financial exploitation of older persons by fraudulent opportunists;
(j) Raise awareness and protect older persons from physical, psychological, sexual or financial abuse in emergency situations, paying particular attention to the specific risks faced by women;
(k) Encourage a more targeted inclusion of older refugees in all aspects of programme planning and implementation, inter alia, by helping active persons to be more self-supporting and by promoting better community care initiatives for the very old;

(l) Enhance international cooperation, including burden-sharing and coordination of humanitarian assistance to countries affected by natural disasters and other humanitarian emergencies and post-conflict situations in ways that would be supportive of recovery and long-term development.

56. **Objective 2: Enhanced contributions of older persons to the re-establishment and reconstruction of communities and the rebuilding of the social fabric following emergencies.**

Actions

(a) Include older persons in the provision of community relief and rehabilitation programmes, including by identifying and helping vulnerable older persons;
(b) Recognise the potential of older persons as leaders in the family and community for education, communication and conflict resolution;
(c) Assist older persons to re-establish economic self-sufficiency through rehabilitation projects, including income generation, educational programmes and occupational activities, taking into account the special needs of older women;
(d) Provide legal advice and information to older persons in situations of displacement and dispossession of land and other productive and personal assets;
(e) Provide special attention for older persons in humanitarian aid programmes and packages offered in situations of natural disasters and other humanitarian emergencies;
(f) Share and apply, as appropriate, lessons learned from practices that have successfully utilised the contributions of older persons in the aftermath of emergencies.

B. Regional forums

I. Council of Europe

Parliamentary Assembly recommendation 1619 (2003) rights of elderly migrants, 8 September 2003

1. People over 55 years of age represent a noticeable proportion of the immigrant population of Council of Europe member states. Arriving in the 1950s and 1960s, following the economic boom in some western European countries, or as a result of decolonisation movements, they have settled, worked and lived most of their lives in Council of Europe member states. Some of them have a history of hard physical labour or bad working conditions; others come from countries with low life expectancy; others have experienced stress due to racism, discrimination or poverty. Due to their past experience and age, these migrants can be considered as elderly. Their number is due to increase in the next decades, given the ageing of the population, including the population of migrant origin, in traditional immigration countries. Council of Europe member states which are new immigration countries will soon experience the same phenomenon.
2. The Parliamentary Assembly recalls its previous texts in the fields of the ageing population and social care and social security, including Recommendations 761 (1975) on payments of pensions in cases of mixed careers and on the establishment of a European passport of social security, 1573 (2002) on the ratification of the European Code of Social Security, 1254 (1994) on medical and welfare rights of the elderly: ethics and politics, and Resolution 1008 (1993) on social policies for elderly persons and their self-reliance. The Assembly also recalls the European Convention on Social Security (ETS No. 78) and its Supplementary Agreement for the Application of the European Convention on Social Security (ETS No. 78A), and regrets that, to date, this convention has been ratified by only eight Council of Europe member states and signed by an additional five.
3. The Assembly is convinced that a coherent policy is needed to address the situation of elderly migrants in Council of Europe member states, whether they wish to remain in the host country or go back to their countries of origin. Comprehensive action should be conducted at political and legislative level to protect the rights of elderly migrants, ensure their social inclusion and well-being at a delicate stage of their life, and make sure that they are not subjected to a dual discrimination, both as elderly people and as migrants.
4. The Assembly therefore recommends that the Committee of Ministers:
   4.1. instruct its relevant committees to conduct research into the situation of elderly migrants in Council of Europe member states.

Such research should embrace aspects such as demography, social inclusion, legal status, pension and other social rights;

4.2. call on member states to:

a. develop coherent and comprehensive policies to address the situation of elderly migrants, through an inter-departmental approach involving the ministries of labour, immigration, health and social affairs and in consultation with the voluntary sector, community organisations and elderly migrants themselves;

b. promote partnerships with non-governmental organisations and support voluntary initiatives, particularly by earmarking budgetary and other resources and by granting voluntary workers legal status and adequate social protection;

c. sign and ratify the European Convention on Social Security;

d. ensure the transferability of full pension rights for migrant workers, wherever they decide to take up residence;

e. ensure that criteria such as knowledge of the language or the way of life of the host country are interpreted with flexibility when considering naturalisation applications from elderly migrants;

f. adapt the existing structures for the provision of health care and assistance to the elderly to make them culturally appropriate to the needs of elderly migrants, also through the provision of special training to social workers and health professionals;

g. encourage the employment of qualified personnel from an immigrant background in health care and assistance structures;

h. facilitate the access to health care and assistance services through the provision of interpretation upon demand for elderly migrants who are not able to communicate effectively in the language of the host country. This service should be available free of charge for destitute elderly migrants;

i. ensure that council and state housing be made available to meet the requirements of elderly migrants, bearing in mind the needs of homeless families and the particular facilities necessary for them;

j. provide clear information about access to social welfare, pension and health care in the host country and the country of origin and make it accessible to elderly migrants through public institutions as well as community centres, immigrant organisations, cultural centres and religious institutions frequented by immigrants;
k. encourage less elderly migrants to (re-)enter the labour market, if necessary granting access to vocational courses to reconvert skills and competences acquired during their previous work experience;
l. encourage the maintenance of links between elderly immigrants and their countries of origin, among other things through the organisation of cultural events, exhibitions and performing arts events and the support of language courses;
m. encourage cultural and educational activities involving elderly migrants;
n. promote socio-gerontological research for the better understanding of the situation of elderly migrants. https://pace.coe.int/pdf/20602681675bb3fe2a3beccfbbc9cce2254ab04d33ace7ec60019747411381e5?title=Rec.1619.pdf.

II. European Union

Excerpts

Directive 2013/33/EU of the European Parliament and of the Council of 26 June 2013 Laying Down Standards for the Reception of Applicants for International Protection (Recast)

Article 21

General principle

Member States shall take into account the specific situation of vulnerable persons such as minors, unaccompanied minors, disabled people, elderly people, pregnant women, single parents with minor children, victims of human trafficking, persons with serious illnesses, persons with mental disorders and persons who have been subjected to torture, rape or other serious forms of psychological, physical or sexual violence, such as victims of female genital mutilation, in the national law implementing this Directive.

Article 22

Assessment of the special reception needs of vulnerable persons

1. In order to effectively implement Article 21, Member States shall assess whether the applicant is an applicant with special reception needs. Member States shall also indicate the nature of such needs.
   That assessment shall be initiated within a reasonable period of time after an application for international protection is made and may be integrated into existing national procedures. Member States shall ensure that those special reception needs are also addressed, in accordance with the provisions of this Directive, if they become apparent at a later stage in the asylum procedure.
   Member States shall ensure that the support provided to applicants with special reception needs in accordance with this Directive takes into account their special reception needs throughout the duration of the asylum procedure and shall provide for appropriate monitoring of their situation.
2. The assessment referred to in paragraph 1 need not take the form of an administrative procedure.
3. Only vulnerable persons in accordance with Article 21 may be considered to have special reception needs and thus benefit from the specific support provided in accordance with this Directive.
4. The assessment provided for in paragraph 1 shall be without prejudice to the assessment of international protection needs pursuant to Directive 2011/95/EU.

Regulation (EU) 2024/1356 of the European Parliament and of the Council of 14 May 2024 introducing the screening of third-country nationals at the external borders and amending regulations (EC) NO 767/2008, (EU) 2017/2226, (EU) 2018/1240 AND (EU) 2019/817

Recital 38

During the screening, all persons concerned should be guaranteed a standard of living complying with the Charter and have access to emergency health care and essential treatment of illnesses. Particular attention should be paid to individuals with vulnerabilities, such as pregnant women, **elderly**

persons, single-parent families, persons with an immediately identifiable physical or mental disability, persons visibly having suffered psychological or physical trauma and unaccompanied minors. In particular, in the case of a minor, information should be provided in a child-friendly and age-appropriate manner. All the authorities involved in the performance of the tasks related to the screening should report any situation of vulnerabilities observed or reported to them, should respect human dignity and privacy, and should refrain from any discrimination.

Regulation (EU) 2024/1351 of the European Parliament and of the Council of 14 May 2024 on asylum and migration management, amending regulations (EU) 2021/1147 and (EU) 2021/1060 and repealing regulation (EU) NO 604/2013

Article 50

Exchange of health data before a transfer is carried out

For the sole purpose of the provision of medical care or treatment, in particular concerning vulnerable persons, including disabled persons, **elderly people**, pregnant women, minors and persons who have been subject to torture, rape or other serious forms of psychological, physical or sexual violence, the transferring Member State shall, in so far as it is available to its competent authority in accordance with national law, transmit to the Member State responsible information on any special needs of the person to be transferred, which in specific cases can include information on that person's physical or mental health. That information shall be transferred in a common health certificate with the necessary documents attached. The Member State responsible shall ensure that those special needs are adequately addressed, including in particular any essential medical care required.

Regulation (EU) 2024/1348 of the European Parliament and of the Council of 14 May 2024 establishing a common procedure for international protection in the Union and repealing Directive 2013/32/EU

Recital (61)

Pursuant to Chapter IV of Directive (EU) 2024/1346, Member States providing reception facilities for carrying out the asylum border procedure are under an obligation to take into account the special situation and needs of vulnerable persons, including minors, persons with a disability and **elderly people**. Consequently, such persons should only be admitted to a border procedure in the event that the conditions of reception within that procedure comply with the requirements set out in Chapter IV of that Directive. Furthermore, in the event that reception conditions available as part of a border procedure cease to comply with the requirements and standards laid down in Chapter IV of that Directive, the border procedure should cease to apply to the persons concerned.

Regulation (EU) 2024/1359 of the European Parliament and of the Council of 14 May 2024 addressing situations of crisis and *Force Majeure* in the field of migration and asylum and amending regulation (EU) 2021/1147

Recital (37)
Vulnerable persons should be given primary consideration for relocation, in particular when they have special reception needs within the meaning of Article 24 of Directive (EU) 2024/1346, or are in need of special procedural guarantees as referred to in Articles 20 to 23 of Regulation (EU) 2024/1348. According to Article 24 of Directive (EU) 2024/1346, applicants falling within any of the following categories are more likely to have special reception needs: minors, unaccompanied minors, persons with disabilities, elderly persons, pregnant women, lesbian, gay, bisexual, trans and intersex persons, single parents with minor children, victims of trafficking in human beings, persons with serious illnesses, persons with mental disorders including post-traumatic stress disorder and persons who have been subjected to torture, rape or other serious forms of psychological, physical or sexual violence, such as victims of gender-based violence, of female genital mutilation, of child or forced marriage, or violence committed with a sexual, gender, racist or religious motive.

Directive (EU) 2024/1346 of the European Parliament and of the Council of 14 May 2024 laying down standards for the reception of applicants for international protection (Recast)

Article 24
Applicants with special reception needs

Member States shall take into account the specific situation of applicants with special reception needs.

Member States shall take into consideration the fact that certain applicants such as those falling within any of the following categories, are more likely to have special reception needs:

minors;
unaccompanied minors;
persons with disabilities;
elderly persons;
pregnant women;
lesbian, gay, bisexual, trans and intersex persons;
single parents with minor children;
victims of trafficking in human beings;
persons with serious illnesses;
persons with mental disorders including post-traumatic stress disorder;
persons who have been subjected to torture, rape or other serious forms of psychological, physical or sexual violence, for example victims of gender-based violence, of female genital mutilation, of child or forced marriage, or violence committed with a sexual, gender, racist or religious motive.

Article 25
Assessment of special reception needs

1. In order to effectively implement Article 24, Member States shall, as early as possible after an application for international protection is made, individually assess whether the applicant has special reception needs, using oral translation where necessary.

The assessment referred to in the first subparagraph of this paragraph may be integrated into existing national procedures or into the assessment referred to in Article 20 of Regulation (EU) 2024/1348.

The assessment referred to in the first subparagraph of this paragraph shall be initiated by identifying special reception needs based on visible signs or on the applicants' statements or behaviour or, where applicable, statements of the parents or the representative of the applicant.

The assessment referred to in the first subparagraph of this paragraph shall be completed within 30 days from the making of the application for international protection or, where it is integrated into the assessment referred to in Article 20 of Regulation (EU) 2024/1348, within the timeframe set out in that Regulation, and the special reception needs identified on the basis of such assessment shall be addressed.

Where special reception needs become apparent at a later stage in the procedure for international protection, Member States shall assess and address those needs.

Member States shall ensure that the support provided to applicants with special reception needs in accordance with this Directive takes into account their special reception needs throughout the duration of the procedure for international protection and shall provide for appropriate monitoring of their situation.

2. For the purposes of paragraph 1, Member States shall ensure that the staff assessing special reception needs in accordance with this Article:
   (a) are trained and continue to be trained to detect signs that an applicant has special reception needs and to address those needs when identified;
   (b) include information concerning the nature of the applicant's special reception needs in the applicant's file held by the competent authorities, together with a description of the visible signs or the applicants' statements or behaviour relevant for the assessment of the applicants' special reception needs as well as the measures that have been identified to address those needs and the authorities responsible for addressing those needs; and
   (c) subject to prior consent in accordance with national law, refer applicants to the appropriate medical practitioner or psychologist for further assessment of their psychological and physical state where there are indications that their mental or physical health could affect their reception needs; where necessary, oral translation shall be provided by professionals trained in translation to ensure that the applicant is able to communicate with medical staff; where the lack of such trained professionals would risk delaying the treatment, oral translation may be provided by other adult individuals, subject to the applicant's consent.

The competent authorities shall take into account the result of the assessment referred to in point (c) when deciding on the type of special reception support which may be provided to the applicant.

3. The assessment referred to in the first subparagraph of paragraph 1 need not take the form of an administrative procedure.
4. Only applicants with special reception needs may benefit from the specific support provided in accordance with this Directive.
5. The assessment provided for in the first subparagraph of paragraph 1 shall be without prejudice to the assessment of international protection needs pursuant to Regulation (EU) 2024/1347.

Regulation (EU) 2024/1347 of the European Parliament and of the Council of 14 May 2024 on standards for the qualification of third-country nationals or stateless persons as beneficiaries of international protection, for a uniform status for refugees or for persons eligible for subsidiary protection and for the content of the protection granted, amending council directive 2003/109/EC and repealing directive 2011/95/EU of the European Parliament and of the Council

Article 20
General rules

1. Without prejudice to the rights and obligations laid down in the Geneva Convention, beneficiaries of international protection shall have the rights and obligations laid down in this Chapter.
2. Beneficiaries of international protection shall have access to rights provided in accordance with this Chapter once international protection is granted and for as long as refugee status or subsidiary protection status is held.
3. Where a residence permit is not issued to a beneficiary of international protection within 15 days of the granting of international protection, the Member State concerned shall take provisional measures, such as registration or the issuance of a document, to ensure that the beneficiary has effective access to the rights laid down in this Chapter, with the exception of those laid down in Articles 25 and 27, until such time as a residence permit is issued in accordance with Article 24.
4. When applying this Chapter, and where it is established that a person has special needs due to being, for example, a minor, an unaccompanied minor, a person with a disability, **an elderly person**, a pregnant

woman, a single parent with a minor or an adult dependent child, a victim of trafficking in human beings, a person with a serious illness, a person with a mental disorder or a person who has been subjected to torture, rape or other serious forms of psychological, physical or sexual violence, the competent authorities shall take into account those special needs.

III. Organization of American States

The Inter-American convention on protecting the human rights of older persons adopted at the general assembly of the organization of American States in Washington, DC, on 15 June 2015

Excerpts

Article 5
Equality and non-discrimination for reasons of age

This Convention prohibits discrimination based on the age of older persons.

In their policies, plans, and legislation on ageing and old age, States Parties shall develop specific approaches for older persons who are vulnerable and those who are victims of multiple discrimination, including women, persons with disabilities, persons of different sexual orientations and gender identities, migrants, persons living in poverty or social exclusion, people of African descent, and persons pertaining to indigenous peoples, the homeless, people deprived of their liberty, persons pertaining to traditional peoples, and persons who belong to ethnic, racial, national, linguistic, religious, and rural groups, among others.

Article 17
Right to social security

All older persons have the right to social security to protect them so that they can live in dignity.

State Parties shall progressively promote, within available resources, the provision of income to ensure a dignified life for older persons through social security systems and other flexible social protection mechanisms.

States Parties shall seek to facilitate, through institutional agreements, bilateral treaties, and other hemispheric mechanisms, the recognition of benefits, social security contributions, and pension entitlements for migrant older persons.

Everything in this article will be in accordance with national legislation.

IV. African Union

African Union convention for the protection and assistance of internally displaced persons in Africa adopted by the special summit of the union Kampala, Uganda 23rd October 2009 (Kampala Convention)

Excerpt

[...]

Article IX

Obligations of States Parties Relating to Protection And Assistance During Internal Displacement

[...]

2. States Parties shall:

   (a) Take necessary measures to ensure that internally displaced persons are received, without discrimination of any kind and live in satisfactory conditions of safety, dignity and security;
   (b) Provide internally displaced persons to the fullest extent practicable and with the least possible delay, with adequate humanitarian assistance, which shall include food, water, shelter, medical care and other health services, sanitation, education, and any other necessary social services, and where appropriate, extend such assistance to local and host communities;
   (c) Provide special protection for and assistance to internally displaced persons with special needs, including separated and unaccompanied children, female heads of households, expectant mothers, mothers with young children, **the elderly**, and persons with disabilities or with communicable diseases.

References

Bibliography

Abi Chahine, Maya, and Hanna Kienzler. "Ageism, an Invisible Social Determinant of Health for Older Syrian Refugees in Lebanon: A Service Providers' Perspective". *Conflict and Health* 16, no. 1 (24 November 2022): 62. https://doi.org/10.1186/s13031-022-00491-9.

Alebeek, Rosanne van, and Andre Nollkaemper. "The Legal Status of Decisions by Human Rights Treaty Bodies in National Law". In *UN Human Rights Treaty Bodies. Law and Legitimacy Edited by Helen Keller and Geir Ulfstein*, 356–413. Cambridge: Cambridge University Press, 2012.

Askola, Heli. "(No) Migrating for Family Care in Later Life: Senchishak v Finland, Older Parents and Family Reunification". *European Journal of Migration and Law* 18, no. 3 (20 September 2016): 351–72. https://doi.org/10.1163/15718166-12342106.

Barbelet, Veronique. "Older People in Displacement Falling through the Cracks of Emergency Responses". London: HelpAge International, Humanitarian Policy Group, Overseas Development Institute, 2018.

Bator-Bryła, Monika Patrycja. "Prohibition of Discrimination on Grounds of Nationality in the Freedom of Movement of Persons within the EU in the Light of Case Law of the Court of Justice of the European Union". *Review of European and Comparative Law* 46, no. 3 (21 August 2021): 189–218. https://doi.org/10.31743/recl.12340.

Battistella, Graziano. In *Migration and Human Rights: The United Nations Convention on Migrant Workers' Rights*, edited by Ryszard Cholewinski, Antoine Pécoud, and Paul de Guchteneire, 1. publ., 47–69. UNESCO Publishing. Cambridge: Cambridge University Press [u.a.], 2009.

Bolzman, Claudio, and Giacomo Vagni. "Forms of Care among Native Swiss and Older Migrants from Southern Europe: A Comparison". *Journal of Ethnic and Migration Studies* 43, no. 2 (25 January 2017): 250–69. https://doi.org/10.1080/1369183X.2016.1238908.

Botha, Henk. "Human Dignity in Comparative Perspective". *Stellenbosch Law Review* 20, no. 2 (2009): 171–220. http://hdl.handle.net/10019.1/103998.

Camarota, Steven A., and Karen Zeigler. "Immigrants Coming to America at Older Ages. A Look at Age at Arrival among New Immigrants, 2000 to 2019". Washington, D.C.: Center for Immigration Studies, 2021.

Catanzariti, Mariavittoria. "The Juridification of Vulnerability in the European Legal Culture". *Oñati Socio-Legal Series* 12, no. 6 (1 December 2022): 1391–1416. https://doi.org/10.35295/osls.iisl/0000-0000-0000-1314.

Chowdhury, Joie. "Unpacking the Minimum Core and Reasonableness Standards". In *Research Handbook on International Law and Social Rights*, edited by Christina Binder, Jane A. Hofbauer, Flávia Piovesan, and Amaya Úbeda de Torres, 251–74. Cheltenham, UK ; Northampton, Massachusetts, USA: Edward Elgar Publishing Limited, 2020.

Ciobanu, Ruxandra Oana, and Claudio Bolzman. "The Interplay between International Migration and the Welfare State in the Context of the Ageing of the Migrant Population". *Scientific Annals of the Alexandru Ioan Cuza University, Iasi,* 8, no. 2 (2015): 9–31.

Conboy, Patricia. "Older-Age Exclusion and the 2030 Agenda for Sustainable Development". In *Social Exclusion in Later Life Interdisciplinary and Policy Perspectives*, Kieran Walsh, Thomas Scharf, Sofie Van Regenmortel, Anna Wanka,. International Perspectives on Aging. 359–372: Springer Nature, 2021. 030-51406-8 (eBook) https://doi.org/10.1007/978-3-030-51406-8.

Cruz-Martínez, Gibrán. "Rethinking Universalism: Older-Age International Migrants and Social Pensions in Latin America and the Caribbean". *Global Social Policy* 20, no. 1 (April 2020): 39–59. https://doi.org/10.1177/1468018119873267.

Dolberg, Pnina, Sigurveig H. Sigurđardóttir, and Ursula Trummer. "Ageism and Older Immigrants". In *Contemporary Perspectives on Ageism*, edited by Liat Aylon and Clemens Tesh – Romer, 177–91. Cham: Springer, 2018.

Doliwa-Klepacka, Anna. "The New Pact on Migration and Asylum as a Response to Current Migration Challenges – Selected Issues". *Białostockie Studia Prawnicze* 26, no. 1 (1 March 2021): 9–21. https://doi.org/10.15290/bsp.2021.26.01.01.

Doron, Israel, and Gerard Quinn. *Against Ageism and Towards Active Social Citizenship for Older Persons The Current Use and Future Potential of the European Social Charter*. Strasbourg: Council of Europe,

2021. https://rm.coe.int/against-ageism-and-towards-active-social-citizenship-for-older-persons/1680a3f5da.

Drzemczewski, Andrew Z. *European Human Rights Convention in Domestic Law: A Comparative Study.* Oxford University Press, 1983.

Dupré, Catherine. *The Age of Dignity: Human Rights and Constitutionalism in Europe.* Oxford, Portland, Oregon: Hart Publishing, 2015.

Eide, Asbjørn. "Economic and Social Rights". In *Human Rights: Concepts and Standards*, edited by Janusz Symonides, 109–75. Dartmouth: Unesco Publishing/ Ashgate, 2000.

Ekoh, Prince Chiagozie, Anthony Obinna Iwuagwu, Elizabeth Onyedikachi George, and Christine A. Walsh. "Forced Migration-Induced Diminished Social Networks and Support, and Its Impact on the Emotional Wellbeing of Older Refugees in Western Countries: A Scoping Review". *Archives of Gerontology and Geriatrics* 105 (February 2023): 104839. https://doi.org/10.1016/j.archger.2022.104839.

El Tatary, Ghassan, and Neeraj Gill. "The Impact of the COVID-19 Pandemic on the Mental Health and Wellbeing of Refugees and Asylum Seekers-A Narrative Review of the Literature". *Australasian Psychiatry* 30, no. 6 (December 2022): 728–31. https://doi.org/10.1177/10398562221131154.

Erk, Christian. *Health, Rights and Dignity : Philosophical Reflections on an Alleged Human Right.* Paris, Frankfurt, Lancaster, New Brunswick: Ontos Verlag, 2011.

Fennelly, David, and Clíodhna Murphy. "Racial Discrimination and Nationality and Migration Exceptions: Reconciling CERD and the Race Equality Directive". *Netherlands Quarterly of Human Rights* 39, no. 4 (December 2021): 308–28. https://doi.org/10.1177/09240519211055648.

Fineman, Martha Albertson. " 'Elderly' as Vulnerable: Rethinking the Nature of Individual and Societal Responsibility". *SSRN Electronic Journal*, 2012. https://doi.org/10.2139/ssrn.2088159.

Fitzmaurice, Malgosia. "Interpretation of Human Rights Treaties". In *The Oxford Handbook of International Human Rights Law*, edited by Dinah Shelton, 739–71. Oxford: Oxford University Press, 2013.

Flynn, Matt, Petia Genkova, Elaine Dewhurst, and Christoph Daniel Schaefer. "Editorial: Ageing and Migration Status: Intersectional Forms of Discrimination and Exclusion". *Frontiers in Psychology* 14 (21 February 2023): 1150578. https://doi.org/10.3389/fpsyg.2023.1150578.

Fokkema, Tineke, and Ruxandra Oana Ciobanu. "Older Migrants and Loneliness: Scanning the Field and Looking Forward". *European Journal of Ageing* 18, no. 3 (September 2021): 291–97. https://doi.org/10.1007/s10433-021-00646-2.

Fox-Ruhs, Clare, and Martin Ruhs. "The Fundamental Rights of Irregular Migrant Workers in the EU". European Parliament, Policy Department for Citizens' Rights and Constitutional Affairs European Parliament, 2022. https://www.europarl.europa.eu/RegData/etudes/STUD/2022/702670/IPOL_STU(2022)702670_EN.pdf.

Fredman, Sandra. *Intersectional Discrimination in EU Gender Equality and Non-discrimination Law*. LU: Publications Office, 2016. https://data.europa.eu/doi/10.2838/241520.

Fredvang, Marthe, and Simon Biggs. "The Rights of Older Persons. Protection and Gaps under Human Rights Law". Social Policy Working Paper. Brotherhood of St Laurence: Brotherhood of St Laurence, Centre for Public Policy, 2012. https://library.bsl.org.au/jspui/bitstream/1/3179/1/Rights_of_older_persons_MFredvang&SBiggs_2012.pdf.

Freedman, Rosa. "The Human Rights Council". In *The UN and Human Rights: A Critical Appraisal*, edited by Frédéric Mégret and Philip Alston, Second edition, 181–238. New York: Oxford University Press, 2019.

Freedman, Rosa, and Jacob Mchangama. "Expanding or Diluting Human Rights?: The Proliferation of United Nations Special Procedures Mandates". *Human Rights Quarterly* 38, no. 1 (2016): 164–93. https://doi.org/10.1353/hrq.2016.0012.

Gaer, Felice D. "Picking and Choosing? Country Visits by Thematic Special Procedures". In *The United Nations Special Procedures System*, edited by Aoife Nolan, Rosa Freedman, and Thérèse Murphy, 87–130. Brill | Nijhoff, 2017. https://doi.org/10.1163/9789004304703_005.

Gałka, Katarzyna. "Status and Protection of Applicants for International Protection in the European Union with Special Needs as Regards Reception Conditions". In *Human Rights in the European Paradigm of the Protection of Aliens*, edited by Elżbieta Karska, Elżbieta Hanna Morawska, Jakub Czepek, Łukasz Dawid Dąbrowski, Bartłomiej Oręziak, and Katarzyna Gałka. Warsaw, 2023.

Galka, Katarzyna. "Vulnerability and Its Implications: Some Comments in the Light of the Strasbourg Case Law Concerning Asylum Seekers". *Espaço Jurídico Journal of Law [EJJL]* 22, no. 2 (22 December 2021): 285–300. hhttps://www.researchgate.net/publication/359754544_Vulnerability_and_its_implications_some_comments_in_the_light_of_the_Strasbourg_case_law_concerning_asylum_seekers

Gardiner, Richard. *Treaty Interpretation*. Oxford: Oxford University Press, 2015.

Garlicki, Leszek. *Konwencja o Ochronie Praw Człowieka i Podstawowych Wolności. Komentarz, Tom II, [Convention for the Protection of Human Rights and Fundamental Freedoms. Commentary, Volume II], Edited by Leszek Garlicki*. Warsaw: C.H. Beck, 2010.

Griner-Abraham, Véronique. [Growing old in exile: a double punishment or a double luck?]. *Soins. Psychiatrie*, no. 293 (2014): 37–43.

Gutterman, Alan. "Intersectionality and Rights of Older Persons". *SSRN Electronic Journal*, 2023. https://doi.org/10.2139/ssrn.4024373.

Habermas, Jürgen. The Concept of Human Dignity and the Realistic Utopia of Human Rights. *Methaphilosophy* 41, no. 4 (2010): 464–80.

Handbook of Procedures Relating to International Labour Conventions and Recommendations International Labour Standards Department International Labour. Rev. ed. 2012. Geneva: ILO, 2012.

Herring, Jonathan. *Older People in Law and Society*. Oxford: Oxford University Press, 2009.

Holecki, Tomasz, Anna Rogalska, Karolina Sobczyk, Joanna Woźniak-Holecka, and Piotr Romaniuk. Global Elderly Migrations and Their Impact on Health Care Systems. *Frontiers in Public Health* 8 (25 August 2020): 386. https://doi.org/10.3389/fpubh.2020.00386.

Hughes, Glenn. The Concept of Dignity in the Universal Declaration of Human Rights. *The Journal of Religious Ethics* 39, no. 1 (2011): 1–24. http://www.jstor.org/stable/23020122.

Johnson, M Glen, and Janusz Symonides. *The Universal Declaration of Human Rights A History of Its Creation and Implementation 1948–1998*. Paris: UNESCO Publishing, 1998.

Jolkina, Aleksandra. "Migrant Instrumentalisation: Facts and Fictions". *Verfassungsblog: On Matters Constitutional*, 21 September 2023. https://doi.org/10.17176/20230921-223514-0.

Kałduński, Marcin. *Zasada Dobrej Wiary w Prawie Miedzynarodowym [The Good Faith Principle in International Law]*. Monografie Prawnicze. Warsaw: C.H. Beck, 2017.

Kälin, Walter. Supervising the 1951 Convention Relating to the Status of Refugees: Article 35 and Beyond. In *Refugee Protection in International Law: UNHCR's Global Consultations on International Protection*, edited by Volker Türk, Erica Feller, and Frances Nicholson, 613–66. Cambridge University Press, 2003.

Karlberg, Michael. "Reframing Human Dignity". In *Interdisciplinary Perspectives on Human Dignity and Human Rights*, edited by Hoda Mahmoudi Michael L. Penn., 35–48. Bingley: Emerald Publishing Limited, 2020. doi.org/10.1108/978-1-78973-821-620191004.

Karlsson, Sofie Ghazanfareeon, and Jessica H. Jönsson. Forced Migration, Older Refugees and Displacement: Implications for Social Work as a Human Rights Profession. *Journal of Human Rights and Social Work* 5, no. 3 (September 2020): 212–22. https://doi.org/10.1007/s41134-020-00120-6.

Keller, Hellen, and Geir Ulfstein. "Conclusions". In *UN Human Rights Treaty Bodies. Law and Legitimacy*, edited by Helen Keller and Geir Ulfstein, 414–25. Cambridge: Cambridge University Press, 2012.

King, Russell, and Aija Lulle. "Ageing, Migration, and Development". In *Routledge Handbook of Migration and Development*, edited by Tanja Bastia and Ronald Skeldon, 211–20. Routledge International Handbooks. London, New York: Routledge, Taylor & Francis Group, 2020.

King, Russell, Aija Lulle, Dora Sampaio, and Julie Vullnetari. Unpacking the Ageing–Migration Nexus and Challenging the Vulnerability Trope. *Journal of Ethnic and Migration Studies* 43, no. 2 (25 January 2017): 182–98. https://doi.org/10.1080/1369183X.2016.1238904.

Kunkel, Suzanne, J. Scott Brown, Frank J. Whittington, and Jasleen Chahal, eds. *Global Aging: Comparative Perspectives on Aging and the Life Course*. New York: Springer Publishing Company, 2014.

Leijten, Ingrid. *Core Socio-Economic Rights and the European Court of Human Rights. In Core Socio-Economic Rights and the European Court of Human Rights*. Cambridge Studies in European Law and Policy. Cambridge: Cambridge University Press, 2018.

Lewis, Bridget, Kelly Purser, and Kirsty Mackie. *The Human Rights of Older Persons: A Human Rights-Based Approach to Elder Law*. Springer, Singapore, 2020.

Lui Gallassi, Ada, and Lars Harrysson. Sidestepping Rights: An Analysis of the Intersection of Human Rights Obligations and Their Practical Implications for Older Migrants. In *Social Exclusion in Later Life*, edited by Kieran Walsh, Thomas Scharf, Sofie Van Regenmortel, and Anna Wanka, 28:275–86. International Perspectives on Aging. Cham: Springer International Publishing, 2021. https://doi.org/10.1007/978-3-030-51406-8_21.

Mahmoudi, Hoda. "Universal Consciousness of Human Dignity". In *Interdisciplinary Perspectives on Human Dignity and Human Rights*, edited by Hoda Mahmoudi, Michael L. Penn., 17–26. Bingley: Emerald Publishing Limited, 2020. 10.1108/978-1-78973-821-620191002.

Majid, Zeinab, Carly Welch, Justine Davies, and Thomas Jackson. Global Frailty: The Role of Ethnicity, Migration and Socioeconomic Factors. *Maturitas* 139 (September 2020): 33–41. https://doi.org/10.1016/j.maturitas.2020.05.010.

Małecka – Łyszczek, Magdalena, and Radosław Mędrzycki. Axiological Paradigm of Social Inclusion Intensification – Selected Remarks. *Review of European and Comparative Law* XXXVIII (2019): 77–95. https://doi.org/10.31743/recl.4826.

Mantu, Sandra, and Paul Minderhoud. Exploring the Links between Residence and Social Rights for Economically Inactive EU Citizens. *European Journal of Migration and Law* 21, no. 3 (7 August 2019): 313–37. https://doi.org/10.1163/15718166-12340053.

McCrudden, Christopher. Human Dignity and Judicial Interpretation of Human Rights. *European Journal of International Law* 19, no. 4 (2008): 655–724. https://doi.org/10.1093/ejil/chn043.

Mensah, Justice, Amos Mensah, and Aba Mensah Nyameyie. Understanding and Promoting the "Leaving No One behind Ambition Regarding the Sustainable Development Agenda: A Review". *Visegrad Journal on Bioeconomy and Sustainable Development* 11, no. 1 (2022): 6–15. https://doi.org/0.2478/vjbsd-2022-0002.

Mikheieva, Oksana, and Irina Kuznetsova. *Internally Displaced and Immobile People in Ukraine between 2014 and 2022: Older Age and Disabilities as Factors of Vulnerability*. Vol. 77. Migration Research

Series. Geneva: International Organization for Migration, 2023. https://publications.iom.int/books/mrs-no-77-internally-displaced-and-immobile-people-ukraine-between-2014-and-2022-older-age.

Mikołajczyk, Barbara. International Human Rights Law and the Intangible Face of Ageism. *Equality, Diversity and Inclusion: An International Journal* 42, no. 3 (28 March 2023): 434–48. https://doi.org/10.1108/EDI-09-2021-0220.

———. "International Law and Ageism". *Polish Yearbook of International Law* 35 (2015): 83–107. https://czasopisma.inp.pan.pl/index.php/pyil/article/view/2421/2150

———. *Social Inclusion for Older Persons and Human Rights Law. The Potential for Universal and European Instruments*. Wydawnictwo Uniwersytetu Śląskiego, 2023. https://wydawnictwo.us.edu.pl/sites/wydawnictwo.us.edu.pl/files/wus_2023_mikolajczyk_social_inclusion_for_older_persons_ebook.pdf.

Mikołajczyk, Barbara, and Mariusz Jagielski. "'Good Change' and Migration Policy in Poland: In a Trap of Democracy". In *Migrants' Rights, Populism and Legal Resilience in Europe*, edited by Vladislava Stoyanova and Stijn Smet, 1st ed., 236–58. Cambridge University Press, 2022. https://doi.org/10.1017/9781009040396.014.

Mölsä, Mulki, Saija Kuittinen, Marja Tiilikainen, Marja-Liisa Honkasalo, and Raija-Leena Punamäki. Mental Health among Older Refugees: The Role of Trauma, Discrimination, and Religiousness. *Aging & Mental Health* 21, no. 8 (3 August 2017): 829–37. https://doi.org/10.1080/13607863.2016.1165183.

Moya, David, and Georgios Milios, eds. Social Rights and Migrants before the European Court of Human Rights. In *Aliens before the European Court of Human Rights*, 191–210. Brill | Nijhoff, 2021. https://doi.org/10.1163/9789004465695_010.

Muelen, Ruud ter. "Solidarity, Justice, and Recognition of the Other". *Theoretical Medicine and Bioethics*, 37, no. 6 (2016): 517–29. https://doi.org/10.1007/s11017-016-9387-3.

Nagatomo, Jun. *Migration as Transnational Leisure: The Japanese Lifestyle Migrants in Australia*. Social Sciences in Asia 38. Leiden, Boston: Brill, 2014.

Nashwan, Ayat, Sherry M. Cummings, and Kara Gagnon. Older Female Iraqi Refugees in the United States: Voices of Struggle and Strength.

International Social Work 62, no. 2 (March 2019): 653–68. https://doi.org/10.1177/0020872817742699.

Ilcan, Suzan. The Border Harms of Human Displacement: Harsh Landscapes and Human Rights Violations. *Social Sciences* 10, no. 4 (30 March 2021): 123. https://doi.org/10.3390/socsci10040123.

Nowak, Manfred, Karolina Januszewski, and Tina Höffstrater. *All Human Rights for All.* Vienna/Gratz: Insertina, 2012.

O'Flaherty, Michael. The Concluding Observations of United Nations Human Rights Treaty Bodies. *Human Rights Law Review* 6, no. 1 (2006): 27–52.

Oliver, Caroline. "Lifestyle Migration". In *Global Migration Governance*, edited by Alexander Betts, 133–52. Oxford University Press, 2011. https://doi.org/10.1093/acprof:oso/9780199600458.003.0006.

O'Cinneide, Colm. The Human Rights of Migrants with Irregular Status: Giving Substance to Aspirations of Universalism. In *Migrants with Irregular Status in Europe*, edited by Sarah Spencer and Anna Triandafyllidou, 51–71. IMISCOE Research Series. Cham: Springer International Publishing, 2020. https://doi.org/10.1007/978-3-030-34324-8_4.

O'Connell, Paul. *Vindicating Socio-Economic Rights: International Standards and Comparative Experiences*. Routledge Research in Human Rights Law. Milton Park, Abingdon, Oxon, New York: Routledge, 2012.

Palander, Jaana. Recognizing Insecurities of Family Members Abroad: Human Rights Balancing in European and Finnish Case Law. In *Forced Migration and Separated Families*, edited by Marja Tiilikainen, Johanna Hiitola, Abdirashid A. Ismail, and Jaana Palander, 43–60. IMISCOE Research Series. Cham: Springer International Publishing, 2023. https://doi.org/10.1007/978-3-031-24974-7_3.

Palmer, Ellie. Protecting Socio-Economic Rights Through the European Convention on Human Rights: Trends and Developments in the European Court of Human Rights. *Erasmus Law Review* 2, no. 4 (2009): 397–425. https://papers.ssrn.com/sol3/papers.cfm?abstract_id=1542674.

Pariotti, Elena. "Vulnerability and Human Rights: Which Compatibility?" *International Journal for the Semiotics of Law – Revue Internationale de Sémiotique Juridique* 36, no. 4 (August 2023): 1401–13. https://doi.org/10.1007/s11196-023-09977-y.

Pattillo, Mia, Sigsten Stieglitz, Konstantinos Angoumis, and Nora Gottlieb. Racism against Racialized Migrants in Healthcare in Europe: A Scoping Review. *International Journal for Equity in Health* 22, no. 1 (29 September 2023): 201. https://doi.org/10.1186/s12939-023-02014-1.

Peters-Nehrenheim, Viktoria, Mike Rommerskirch-Manietta, Daniel Purwins, Martina Roes, and Hürrem Tezcan-Güntekin. Care Preferences of Older Migrants and Minority Ethnic Groups with Various Care Needs: A Protocol for a Scoping Review. *BMJ Open* 12, no. 11 (November 2022): e061712. https://doi.org/10.1136/bmjopen-2022-061712.

Picker, Eduard. *Godność człowieka a życie ludzkie*. Warszawa: Oficyna Naukowa, 2007.

Piotrowicz, Karolina, Solomiia Semeniv, Robert Kupis, Monika Ryś, Ian Perera, Barbara Gryglewska, and Jerzy Gąsowski. Disease Burden in Older Ukrainian Refugees of War: A Synthetic Reanalysis of Public Records Data. *The Lancet Healthy Longevity* 3, no. 10 (October 2022): e667–73. https://doi.org/10.1016/S2666-7568(22)00187-8.

Powell, Jason L. *Globalization and Global Aging*. New York: Novinka, 2013.

Redondo, Elvira Domínguez. Rethinking the Legal Foundations of Control in International Human Rights Law – The Case of Special Procedures. *Netherlands Quarterly of Human Rights* 29, no. 3 (September 2011): 261–88. https://doi.org/10.1177/016934411102900302.

Reid, Natasha, Shavini Weerasekera, Ruth E. Hubbard, and Emily H. Gordon. "Frailty in Ethnic Minority Women". *Maturitas* 152 (October 2021): 26–31. https://doi.org/10.1016/j.maturitas.2021.07.005.

Repetti, Marion, Christopher Phillipson, and Toni Calasanti. Retirement Migration in Europe: A Choice for a Better Life? *Sociological Research Online* 23, no. 4 (December 2018): 780–94. https://doi.org/10.1177/1360780418782243.

Rosen, Michael. *Dignity. Its History and Meaning*. Cambridge, MA and London: Harvard University Press, 2012.

RosNET. Multidimensional Social Exclusion in Later Life: Briefing Paper and a Roadmap for Future Collaborations in Research and Policy. In K. Walsh and T. Scharf (Series Eds.), *ROSEnet Briefing Paper Series: No. 6. CA 15122 Reducing Old-Age Exclusion: Collaborations in Research and Policy*, 2020. http://rosenetcost.com/wp-content/uploads/2017/01/cost_rosenet_actionpolicy6_web.pdf.

Sampaio, Dora. A Place to Grow Older … Alone? Living and Ageing as a Single Older Lifestyle Migrant in the Azores. *Area* 50, no. 4 (December 2018): 459–66. https://doi.org/10.1111/area.12414.

Scheinin, Martin. "Core Rights and Obligations". In *The Oxford Handbook of International Human Rights Law*, edited by Dinah Shelton, 527–40. Oxford: Oxford University Press, 2013.

Sciaccaluga, Giovanni. Why States Should Protect Forced Climate Migrants. In *International Law and the Protection of "Climate Refugees"*, by Giovanni Sciaccaluga, 129–41. Cham: Springer International Publishing, 2020. https://doi.org/10.1007/978-3-030-52402-9_9.

Shultziner, Doron, and Guy E. Carmi. Human Dignity in National Constitutions: Functions, Promises and Danger. *The American Journal of Comparative Law* 62, no. 2 (2014): 461–90.

Sidani, Souraya, Melissa Northwood, Bharati Sethi, Zhixi Cecilia Zhuang, and Konain Edhi. Social Isolation and Loneliness in Older Immigrants during COVID-19: A Scoping Review. *International Journal of Migration, Health and Social Care* 18, no. 2 (31 May 2022): 164–78. https://doi.org/10.1108/IJMHSC-08-2021-0071.

Siddiq, Hafifa, Qais Alemi, and Eunice Lee. A Qualitative Inquiry of Older Afghan Refugee Women's Individual and Sociocultural Factors of Health and Health Care Experiences in the United States. *Journal of Transcultural Nursing* 34, no. 2 (March 2023): 143–50. https://doi.org/10.1177/10436596221149692.

Smith, Rhona K. M. States of Denial: Rationalising UK Government Responses to UN Special Procedures. *Human Rights Law Review* 21, no. 2 (12 March 2021): 458–74. https://doi.org/10.1093/hrlr/ngaa049.

Spanier, Benny, Israel Doron, and Faina Milman-Sivan. 'Older Persons' Use of the European Court of Human Rights. *Journal of Cross Cultural Gerontology* 28 (2013): 407–20. https://doi.org/10.1007/s10823-013-9212-7.

Stefanovska, Vesna. Retrospective of the Dynamic and Evolutive Interpretation of ECHR: Framing the Strasbourg's Interpretative Ethic. *Iustinianus Primus Law Review* 11, no. 1 (2020): 1–11.

Stewart, Melissa. 'A New Law on Earth' Hannah Arendt and the Vision for a Positive Legal Framework to Guarantee the Right to Have Rights. *SSRN Electronic Journal*, 2021. https://doi.org/10.2139/ssrn.3791785.

Suen, Yiu Tung. Ageing Non-Heterosexual Migrants: Towards Global Sexual Citizenship. *Journal of Aging Studies* 60 (March 2022): 100980. https://doi.org/10.1016/j.jaging.2021.100980.

Sun, Pinghua. P. C. Chang's Concept of Human Dignity for the Universal Declaration of Human Rights. *Journal of East Asia & International Law*. 12, no. 1 (2019). https://doi.org/10.14330/jeail.2019.12.1.05.

Świątkowski, Andtrzej Marian, and Macin Wujczyk. Karta Praw Społecznych Rady Europy Jako Szansa Ustanowienia Jednolitej Koncepcji Obywatelstwa Unii Europejskiej [The Council of Europe's Charter of Social Rights as an Opportunity to Establish a Uniform Concept of European Union Citizenship]. *Roczniki Administracji i Prawa* XVI, no. 2 (2016): 409–36. http://cejsh.icm.edu.pl/cejsh/element/bwmeta1.element.desklight-f847bd20-3aff-4a65-8de4-a11fa6747b78.

Sychenko, Elena. Enlarging the Scope of the European Convention on Human Rights: History, Philosophical Roots and Practical Outcomes. *Zbornik Pravnog Fakulteta u Zagrebu* 65, no. 2 (2015): 309–26. https://www.scopus.com/record/display.uri?eid=2-s2.0-84938949059&origin=inward&txGid=720db1608d11cd12d443900599582c43.

Taylor, Robert Joseph. Race and Mental Health Among Older Adults: Within- and Between-Group Comparisons. *Innovation in Aging* 4, no. 5 (1 September 2020): igaa056. https://doi.org/10.1093/geroni/igaa056.

Torres, Sandra, and Alistair Hunter, eds. *Handbook on Migration and Ageing*. Elgar Handbooks in Migration. Cheltenham, UK; Northampton, MA, USA: Edward Elgar Publishing, 2023.

Tsourdi, Evangelia (Lilian), and Cathryn Costello. 'Systemic Violations' in EU Asylum Law: Cover or Catalyst? *German Law Journal* 24, no. 6 (September 2023): 982–94. https://doi.org/10.1017/glj.2023.59.

Ulfstein, Geir. "Individual Complaints". In *UN Human Rights Treaty Bodies. Law and Legitimacy Edited by Helen Keller and Geir Ulfstein*, 73–115. Cambridge: Cambridge University Press, 2012.

Verdú Baeza, Jesús. Climate Refugees, Human Rights and the Principle of Non-Refoulement. *Paix et Securite Internationales*, no. 11 (2023). https://doi.org/10.25267/Paix_secur_int.2023.i11.1401.

Villiger, Mark E. *Commentary on the 1969 Vienna Convention on the Law of Treaties*. London: Brill/Nijhof, 2009.

Walsh, Kieran, Thomas Scharf, and Norah Keating. Social Exclusion of Older Persons: A Scoping Review and Conceptual Framework. *European Journal of Ageing* 14, no. 1 (March 2017): 81–98. https://doi.org/10.1007/s10433-016-0398-8.

Wells, Jo. The Neglected Generation the Impact of Displacement on Older People. HelpAge International, 2013. https://www.refworld.org/docid/524571814.html.

Westwood, Sue, ed. *Ageing, Diversity and Equality*. Routledge Advances in Sociology. London: Routledge, 2019.

Wheatley, Steven. *The Idea of International Human Rights Law*. 1st ed. Oxford University Press, 2019. https://doi.org/10.1093/oso/9780198749844.001.0001.

Willekens, Frans J. Demographic Transitions in Europe and the World. 0 ed. Rostock: Max Planck Institute for Demographic Research, March 2014. https://doi.org/10.4054/MPIDR-WP-2014-004.

Wujczyk, Macin. Procedura Skarg Zbiorowych Jako Instrument Ochrony Praw Socjalnych [The Collective Complaints Procedure as an Instrument of Protection of Social Rights]. In *Europejska Karta Społeczna: Wyzwania i Możliwości 25. Rocznica Przystąpienia Polski Do Rady Europy [The European Social Charter: Challenges and Opportunities 25th Anniversary of Poland's Membership of the Council of Europe] Edited by Lesław Nawacki, Anna Szałek, Marcin Wujczyk*, 154–66. Warsaw, 2016.

Zhang, Xuelian. On the Concluding Observations of the United Nations Human Rights Treaty Bodies. *Journal of Human Rights* 18, no. 3 (2019): 351–64.

Treaties

International Labour Organization

Maintenance of Migrants' Pension Rights Convention No. 48, 4 June 1935. https://www.ilo.org/dyn/normlex/en/f?p=NORMLEXPUB:12100:0::NO:12100:P12100_INSTRUMENT_ID:312193:NO.

Migration for Employment Convention (Revised), No. 97, 8 June 1949. https://www.ilo.org/dyn/normlex/en/f?p=NORMLEXPUB:55:0::NO::P55_TYPE,P55_LAN, P55_DOCUMENT,P55_NODE:CON,en, C097,/Document.

The Social Security (Minimum Standards) Convention (No. 102)', 4 June 1952. https://www.ilo.org/dyn/normlex/en/f?p=NORMLEXPUB:12100:0::NO:12100:P12100_INSTRUMENT_ID:312247:NO.

Convention No. 118, Equality of Treatment (Social Security), 6 June 1962. https://www.ilo.org/dyn/normlex/en/f?p=NORMLEXPUB:12100:0::NO::P12100_INSTRUMENT_ID:312263.

Convention No. 128 on Invalidity, Old-Age and Survivors' Benefits Convention, 7 June 1967. https://www.ilo.org/dyn/normlex/en/f?p=NORMLEXPUB:12100:0::NO::P12100_INSTRUMENT_ID:312273.

Convention Concerning Migrations in Abusive Conditions and the Promotion of Equality of Opportunity and Treatment of Migrant Workers, No. 143, 4 June 1975. https://www.ilo.org/dyn/normlex/en/f?p=NORMLEXPUB:55:0::NO::P55_TYPE,P55_LANG,P55_DOCUMENT,P55_NODE:CON,en,C097,/Document.

Maintenance of Social Security Rights Convention, (No. 157), 2 June 1982. https://www.ilo.org/dyn/normlex/en/f?p=NORMLEXPUB:12100:0::NO:12100:P12100_INSTRUMENT_ID:312302:NO.

United Nations

Geneva Convention Relative to the Protection of Civilian Persons in Time of War (Fourth Geneva Convention), 12 August 1949, UNTS vol. 75, p. 287.

Convention Relating to the Status of Refugees, 28 July 1951, UNTS vol. 189, p. 137.

Convention Relating to the Status of Stateless Persons New York, 28 September 1954, UNTS vol. 360, p. 117.

Convention on the Elimination of All Forms of Discrimination a Racial Discrimination (adopted by the UNGA resolution 2106 (XX) 21 December 1965), New York, 7 March December 1966, UNTS vol. 660, p. 195.

International Covenant on Economic, Social and Cultural Rights, New York, 16 December 1966, UNTS, vol. 993, p. 3.

International Covenant on Civil and Political Rights, New York, 16 December 1966, UNTS, vol. 999, p. 171 and vol. 1057, p. 407.

Protocol Relating to the Status of Refugees, 31 January 1967, UNTS, vol. 606, p. 267.

Vienna Convention on the Law of Treaties, 29 May 1969, UNTS, vol. 1155, p. 331.

Convention on the Elimination of All Forms of Discrimination against Women, New York, 18 December 1979, UNTS, vol. 1249, p. 13.

Convention against Torture and Other Cruel, Inhuman or Degrading Treatment or Punishment, New York, 10 December 1984, UNTS, vol. 1465, p. 85.

International Convention on the Protection of the Rights of All Migrant Workers and Members of Their Families, New York, 18 December 1990, UNTS, vol. 2220, p. 3.

Convention on the Rights of Persons with Disabilities, New York, 13 December 2006, UNTS, 2515, vol. 2515, p. 3.

Optional Protocol to the Convention on the Rights of Persons with Disabilities, New York, 13 December 2006, UNTS, vol. 2518, p. 283.

Optional Protocol to the Convention against Torture and Other Cruel, Inhuman or Degrading Treatment or Punishment, New York, 18 December 2002, UNTS 2006, vol. 2375, p. 237.

Optional Protocol to the International Covenant on Economic, Social and Cultural Rights, New York, 10 December 2008, Doc. A/63/435; C.N.869.200

African Union

African Union Convention for the Protection and Assistance of Internally Displaced Persons in Africa ("Kampala Convention"), 23 October 2009, https://www.refworld.org/docid/4ae572d82.html.

Protocol to the African Charter on Human And Peoples – Rights on the Rights of Older Persons in Africa of 31 January 2016, https://au.int/en/treaties/protocol-african-charter-human-and-peoples-rights-rights-older-persons.

Council of Europe

Convention for the Protection of Human Rights and Fundamental Freedoms, Rome, 4 November 1950, European Treaty Series No. 005.

European Social Charter, Turin 18 October 1961, European Treaty Series – No. 035.

European Convention on the Legal Status of Migrant Workers, Strasbourg, 24 November 1977, European Treaty Series – No. 093.

European Convention for the Prevention of Torture and Inhuman or Degrading Treatment or Punishment, Strasbourg 26 November, 1987, European Treaty Series – No. 126.

Protocol Amending the European Social Charter, Turin, 21 October 1991, European Treaty Series – No. 142.

Additional Protocol to the European Social Charter Providing for a System of Collective Complaints, Strasbourg, 9 November 1995, European Treaty Series No. 158

European Social Charter (Revised), Strasbourg, 3 May1996, Council of Europe Treaty Series – No. 163.

Protocol No. 12 to the Convention for the Protection of Human Rights and Fundamental Freedoms, Rome, 4 November, Council of Europe Treaty Series No. 177.

Organization of African Unity

African Charter on Human and Peoples' Rights (Banjul Charter) Adopted 27 June 1981, Doc. CAB/LEG/67/3 Rev. 5, 21. 21 International Legal Materials 58, 1981. https://www.achpr.org/legalinstruments/detail?id=49.

Organization of American States

American Convention on Human Rights, "Pact of San Jose," Costa Rica, 22 November 1969, (B-32)

Inter-American Convention on Protecting the Human Rights of Older Persons adopted at the General Assembly of the Organization of

American States in Washington, DC, on June 15, 2015, http://www.oas.org/en/sla/dil/docs/inter_american_treaties_A-70_human_rights_older_persons.pdf.

Other treaties

Agreement on the withdrawal of the United Kingdom of Great Britain and Northern Ireland from the European Union and the European Atomic Energy Community, O. J. C 384I, 12.11.2019, p. 1–177, https://eur-lex.europa.eu/legal-content/EN/TXT/?uri=CELEX%3A12019W/TXT%2802%29.

Jurisprudence

Court of Justice of the European Union

Judgment of the Court of 26 July 2011 in Case E-4/11 — *Arnulf Clauder*, O. J. C, C/344, 24.11.2011, p. 9, https://eur-lex.europa.eu/legal-content/EN/TXT/?uri=CELEX:E2011J0004).

European Court of Human Rights

M.S.S. v. Belgium and Greece, Application No. 30696/09, Judgement 21 January 2011 (Grand Chamber).

Petrovna Chvzhevska v. Sweden, Application No. 60794/11, Decision, 25 September 2012, 2012.

Pichkur v. Ukraine, Application No. 10441/06, Judgement 7 November 2013, (Final 07 February 2014)", 2013.

Rimma Frolova, v. Finland, Application No. 47772/11, Decision, 14 January 2014, 2014.

Senchishak v. Finland, Application No. 5049/12, Judgement, 18 November 2014 (Final 23 March 2015), 2014.

Verein KlimaSeniorinnen Schweiz and Others v. Switzerland, Application no. 53600/20; Judgement 9 April 2024 (Grand Chamber).

European Commission on Human Rights

Austria v. Italy, Application, No. 788/60, (1961).

Inter-American Court of Human Rights

Advisory Opinion Oc-2/82 of September 24, 1982. The Effect of Reservations on the Entry into Force of the American Convention on Human Rights (Arts. 74 and 75) Requested By The Inter-American Commission On Human Rights (Inter-American Court of Human Rights 1982), https://www.corteidh.or.cr/docs/opiniones/seriea_02_ing.pdf

Resolutions, recommendations and other soft documents

International Labour Organization

Older Workers Recommendation (No. 162) Adopted on 3 June 1980 by the General Conference of the International Labour Organisation, https://www.ilo.org/dyn/normlex/en/f?p=NORMLEXPUB:12100:0::NO::P12100_ILO_CODE:R162.

United Nations General Assembly

Universal Declaration of Human Rights Adopted by the United Nations General Assembly in Paris on 10 December 1948 General Assembly Resolution 217 A. https://documents.un.org/doc/resolution/gen/nr0/043/88/pdf/nr004388.pdf.

Declaration on Territorial Asylum, 14 December 1967, A/RES/2312(XXII), 1967. https://www.refworld.org/docid/3b00f05a2c.html. df.

Vienna International Plan of Action on Ageing, Report of the World Assembly on Ageing, Vienna, 26 July–6 August 1982, General Assembly Resolution 37/51, Question on Ageing, https://www.un.org/esa/socdev/ageing/documents/Resources/VIPEE-English.pdf.

United Nations Principles for Older Persons Adopted 16 December 1991, A/RES/46/91, https://undocs.org/A/RES/46/91.

Resolution of 16 October 1992 Proclamation on Ageing, A/RES/47/5https://www.un.org/development/desa/ageing/resources/international-year-of-older-persons-1999/resolution-475.html.

World Conference Against Racism, Racial Discrimination, Xenophobia and Related Intolerance. Declaration and Programme of Action, Durban, 31 August-7 September 2001, https://www.ohchr.org/sites/default/files/Documents/Publications/Durban_text_en.pdf.

Madrid International Plan of Action on Ageing and the Political Declaration, Report of the Second World Assembly on Ageing, Madrid, 8–12 April 2002 (United Nations Publication, Sales No. E.02.IV.4), https://www.un.org/development/desa/ageing/madrid-plan-of-action-and-its-implementation.html.

Transforming Our World: The 2030 Agenda for Sustainable Development, Resolution Adopted by the General Assembly on 25 September 2015, A/RES/70/1, https://www.unfpa.org/resources/transforming-our-world-2030-agenda-sustainable-development.

New Urban Agenda, Resolution Adopted by the General Assembly on 23 December 2016 A/RES/71/256, https://habitat3.org/wp-content/uploads/New-Urban-Agenda-GA-Adopted-68th-Plenary-N1646655-E.pdf.

Global Compact on Refugees Adopted by the General Assembly Resolution, 17 December 2018 A/RES/73/151, https://globalcompactrefugees.org/sites/default/files/2019-12/Global%20compact%20on%20refugees%20EN.pdf

Resolution Adopted by the General Assembly. Global Compact for Safe, Orderly and Regular Migration, 19 December 2018, A/RES/73/195. https://documents-dds-ny.un.org/doc/UNDOC/GEN/N18/451/99/PDF/N1845199.pdf?OpenElement.

Human Rights Council

Code of Conduct for Special Procedures Mandate-Holders of the Human Rights Council. A/HCR/RES/5/2, 2007.

Institution-Building of the United Nations Human Rights Council Resolution A/HRC/RES/5/1, 18 June 2007, https://ap.ohchr.org/documents/dpage_e.aspx?si=a/hrc/res/5/1.

Resolution Adopted by the Human Rights Council on 22 June 2017 35/17. Protection of the Human Rights of Migrants: The Global Compact for Safe, Orderly and Regular Migration, 6 July 2017, A/HRC/RES/35/17, https://www.un.org/en/development/desa/population/migration/generalassembly/docs/globalcompact/A_HRC_RES_35_17.pdf.

Resolution Human Rights of Older Persons Adopted by the Human Rights Council on 7 October 2021, A/HRC/RES/48/3, https://documents-dds-ny.un.org/doc/UNDOC/GEN/G21/287/79/PDF/G2128779.pdf?OpenElement.

Human Rights Treaty Bodies

Committee on the Protection of the Rights of All Migrant Workers and Members of Their Families

General Comment No. 5 (2021) on Migrants' Rights to Liberty and Freedom from Arbitrary Detention and Their Connection with Other Human Rights, 21 July 2021, CMW/C/GC/5, https://www.ohchr.org/en/documents/general-comments-and-recommendations/general-comment-no-5-2021-migrants-rights-liberty.

CEDAW Committee

General Recommendation No. 25 on Article 4, Paragraph 1, of the Convention (Temporary Special Measures), 2004. https://tbinternet.ohchr.org/_layouts/15/treatybodyexternal/TBSearch.aspx?Lang=en&TreatyID=3&DocTypeID=11.

General Recommendation No. 27 on Older Women and Protection of Their Human Rights, CEDAW/C/GC/27, 2010. https://documents-dds-ny.un.org/doc/UNDOC/GEN/G10/472/53/PDF/G1047253.pdf?OpenElement.

General Recommendation No. 28 on the Core Obligations of States Parties under Article 2 of the Convention on the Elimination of All Forms of Discrimination against Women, CEDAW/C/GC/28", 2010. https://undocs.org/CEDAW/C/GC/28.

Committee on Economic Social and Cultural Rights

Committee on Economic Social and Cultural Rights. General Comment No. 3: The Nature of States Parties' Obligations (Art. 2, Para. 1, of the Covenant), 1990. https://tbinternet.ohchr.org/_layouts/15/treatybodyexternal/Download.aspx?symbolno=INT%2fCESCR%2fGEC%2f4758&Lang=en.

General Comment No. 6: The Economic, Social and Cultural Rights of Older Persons, E/1996/22, 8 December 1995. https://www.refworld.org/docid/4538838f11.html.

General Comment No. 20: Non-Discrimination in Economic, Social and Cultural Rights (Art. 2, Para. 2, of the International Covenant on

Economic, Social and Cultural Rights, E/C.12/GC/20, 2009. https://www.refworld.org/docid/4a60961f2.html.

General Comment No. 24 (2017) on State Obligations under the International Covenant on Economic, Social and Cultural Rights in the Context of Business Activities, E/C.12/GC/24, 2017. https://tbinternet.ohchr.org/_layouts/15/treatybodyexternal/Download.aspx?symbolno=INT%2fCESCR%2fGEC%2f4758&Lang=en.

Committee on the Elimination of Racial Discrimination

General Recommendation 30, Discrimination against Non-Citizens, 64th Session, 23 February-12 March 2004, CERD/C/64/Misc.11/Rev.3, https://www.google.com/url?sa=t&rct=j&q=&esrc=s&source=web&cd=&ved=2ahUKEwip2vf55dODAxWwKBAIHQ-cDb8QFnoECBEQAQ&url=https%3A%2F%2Fwww2.ohchr.org%2Fenglish%2Fbodies%2Fcerd%2Fdocs%2Fcerd-gc30.doc&usg=AOvVaw3yedj6egtj76SvAuyFH-ic&opi=89978449.

Committee on the Rights of Persons with Disabilities

General Comment No. 6 (2018) on Equality and Non-Discrimination, CRPD/C/GC/6, 2018. https://tbinternet.ohchr.org/_layouts/15/TreatyBodyExternal/TBSearch.aspx?Lang=en&TreatyID=4&DocTypeCategoryID=7.

Human Rights Committee

General Comment No. 15: The Position of Aliens Under the Covenant, 11 April 1986, https://www.refworld.org/docid/45139acfc.html.

General Comment No. 31. The Nature of the General Legal Obligation Imposed on States Parties to the Covenant Adopted on 29 March 2004 (2187th Meeting), CCPR/C/21/Rev.1/Add. 13, 2004. https://digitallibrary.un.org/record/533996.

Regional soft law and other documents

Council of Europe. Explanatory Report to the Protocol No. 12 to the Convention for the Protection of Human Rights and Fundamental

Freedoms, Rome, 4 November 2000, Council of Europe Treaty Series No. 177, 2000.

Council of Europe. Action Plan on Protecting Vulnerable Persons in the Context of Migration and Asylum in Europe (2021–2025), 2021. https://edoc.coe.int/en/refugees/10241-council-of-europe-action-plan-on-protecting-vulnerable-persons-in-the-context-of-migration-and-asylum-in-europe-2021-2025.html.

CoE PACE. Parliamentary Assembly Recommendation Rights of Elderly Migrants 1619 (2003), 9 August 2003", 2003. https://assembly.coe.int/nw/xml/XRef/Xref-XML2HTML-en.asp?fileid=17137&lang=en.

CoE PACE. Resolution 1509 (2006) on Human Rights of Irregular Migrants, 2006, https://assembly.coe.int/nw/xml/xref/xref-xml2html-en.asp?fileid=17456.

CoE Committee of Ministers. Council of Europe Committee of Recommendation CM/Rec(2011)5 of the Committee of Ministers to Member States on Reducing the Risk of Vulnerability of Elderly Migrants and Improving Their Welfare, 2011. https://www.coe.int/t/democracy/migration/ressources/recommendations-resolutions_en.asp.

CoE Committee of Ministers Recommendation CM/Rec(2014)2 Adopted by the Committee of Ministers of the Council of Europe on 19 February 2014. https://rm.coe.int/1680695bce.

CoE Committee of Ministers. Supervision of The Execution of Judgments and Decisions of the European Court of Human Rights. 14th Annual Report of the Committee of Ministers. Strasbourg, March 2021. https://rm.coe.int/2020-cm-annual-report-eng/1680a1f4e8.

CoE Steering Committee for Human Rights, Steering Committee for Human Rights, Report on the Implementation of the Committee of Ministers' Recommendation CM/Rec (2014) 2 on the Promotion of Human Rights of Older Persons Adopted by the CDDH at Its 90th Meeting (27–30 November 2018), CDDH(2018)R90 Addendum 07/01/2019 (Council of Europe, 2019), https://rm.coe.int/steering-committee-for-human-rights-cddh-cddh-report-on-the-implementa/1680906e2f.

OAS. Inter-American Program for the Promotion and Protection of the Human Rights of Migrants, Including Migrant Workers and Their Families, (June 7, 2005), AG/RES. 2141 (XXXV-O/05). http://rialnet.org/sites/default/files/AG-RES_2141_XXXV-O-05_eng.pdf.

Human Rights Council procedures

Independent Expert on the enjoyment of all human rights by older persons

Report of the Independent Expert on the Enjoyment of All Human Rights by Older Persons, Visit to Austria, A/HRC/30/43/Add.2, 2015. https://uhri.ohchr.org/en/document/242c199a-4c80-41ed-bc0e-b1e1c0b36d3c.

Report of the Independent Expert on the Enjoyment of All Human Rights by Older Persons, Visit to Mozambique A/HRC/42/43/ADD.2. Human Rights Council, 2019. https://uhri.ohchr.org/en/document/ba0cd581-3c27-47c4-ae2b-67861c434ee7.

Report of the Independent Expert on the Enjoyment of All Human Rights by Older Persons, Visit to the Dominican Republic, A/HRC/54/26/Add.3, 2023. https://uhri.ohchr.org/en/document/56705239-99b7-4c9d-ac49-ecf7d3487b5f

Impact of the Coronavirus Disease (COVID-19) on the Enjoyment of All Human Rights by Older Persons, Report of the Independent Expert on the Enjoyment of All Human Rights by Older Persons, Claudia Mahler A/75/205, 2020. https://undocs.org/A/75/205).

Report of the Independent Expert on the Enjoyment of All Human Rights by Older Persons 'Older Persons Deprived of Liberty', 13 September 2022, A/HRC/51/27. United Nations General Assembly, 2022. https://www.ohchr.org/en/documents/thematic-reports/ahrc5127-older-persons-deprived-liberty-report-independent-expert.

Report of the Independent Expert on the Enjoyment of All Human Rights, Claudia Malher, 23 July, Human Rights of Older Persons in the Context of Climate Change-Induced Disasters, 25 July 2023 A/78/226. United Nations General Assembly, 2023. https://www.ohchr.org/en/documents/thematic-reports/a78226-human-rights-older-persons-context-climate-change-induced.

Special Rapporteur on the human rights of internally displaced persons

Report of the Special Rapporteur on the Human Rights of Internally Displaced Persons, Cecilia Jimenez-Damary, on Her Visit to Japan, A/

HRC/53/35/Add.1", 2023. https://uhri.ohchr.org/en/document/56705239-99b7-4c9d-ac49-ecf7d3487b5f.

Special Rapporteur on the human rights of migrants

Report of the Special Rapporteur on the Human Rights of Migrants, Felipe González Morales, 19 July 2022, A/77/189. United Nations General Assembly, 2022. https://documents-dds-ny.un.org/doc/UNDOC/GEN/N22/431/49/PDF/N2243149.pdf?OpenElement.

Report of the Special Rapporteur on the Human Rights of Migrants, Felipe González Morales, Protection of the Labour and Human Rights of Migrant Workers, 14 July 2023, A/78/180, United Nations General Assembly, 2023. https://documents-dds-ny.un.org/doc/UNDOC/GEN/N23/207/02/PDF/N2320702.pdf?OpenElement.

Report of the Special Rapporteur on the Promotion and Protection of Human Rights in the Context of Climate Change Promotion and Protection of Human Rights in the Context of Climate Change Mitigation, Loss and Damage and Participation, 22 July 2022, A/77/226, https://documents.un.org/doc/undoc/gen/n23/207/02/pdf/n2320702.pdf?OpenElement.

Mandates of the Special Rapporteur on the Human Rights of Migrants; the Working Group on Arbitrary Detention; the Special Rapporteur on Contemporary Forms of Slavery, Including Its Causes and Consequences and the Special Rapporteur on Trafficking in Persons, Especially Women and Children, 15 December 2023, Ref.: OL OTH 144/2023, 2023. https://spcommreports.ohchr.org/TMResultsBase/DownLoadPublicCommunicationFile?gId=28674.

Report of the Working Group on the Universal Periodic Review, Austria, 9 April 2021, A/HRC/47/12, https://uhri.ohchr.org/en/document/6fb70583-70d1-49b7-b2b7-2d2a7fd448fe.

EU Law

Consolidated Versions of the Treaty on European Union and the Treaty on the Functioning of the European Union Consolidated Version of the Treaty on European Union Consolidated Version of the Treaty on the Functioning of the European Union Protocols Annexes to the Treaty on the Functioning of the European Union Declarations Annexed to the Final Act of the Intergovernmental Conference Which Adopted the

Treaty of Lisbon, Signed on 13 December 2007 Tables of Equivalences. O. J. of the European Union (2016/C 202/01). European Union, 2007. https://eur-lex.europa.eu/legal-content/EN/TXT/?uri=celex%3A12016ME%2FTXT.

Council Directive 2000/43/EC of 29 June 2000 Implementing the Principle of Equal Treatment between Persons Irrespective of Racial or Ethnic Origin. O. J. L 180, 19.7.2000, pp. 22–26. https://eur-lex.europa.eu/legal-content/EN/TXT/?uri=celex%3A32000L0043.

Council Directive 2000/78/EC of 27 November 2000 Establishing a General Framework for Equal Treatment in Employment and Occupation. O. J. L 303, 02/12/2000, p. 16 -22, https://eur-lex.europa.eu/legal-content/EN/TXT/?uri=celex%3A32000L0078.

Council Directive 2001/55/EC of 20 July 2001 on Minimum Standards for Giving Temporary Protection in the Event of a Mass Influx of Displaced Persons and on Measures Promoting a Balance of Efforts between Member States in Receiving Such Persons and Bearing the Consequences Thereof. O. J. L 212, 07.08.2001, pp. 12–23, https://eur-lex.europa.eu/eli/dir/2001/55/oj.

Council Directive 2003/109/EC of 25 November 2003 Concerning the Status of Third-Country Nationals Who Are Long-Term Residents. O. J. L 16, 21.1.2003, pp. 44–53, https://eur-lex.europa.eu/legal-content/EN/TXT/?uri=celex%3A32003L0109.

Regulation (EC) No. 883/2004 of the European Parliament and of the Council of 29 April 2004 on the Coordination of Social Security Systems. O. J. L 166, 30.4.2004, p. 1–126, https://eur-lex.europa.eu/legal-content/PL/TXT/?uri=celex%3A32004L0038.

Directive 2004/38/EC of the European Parliament and of the Council of 29 April 2004 on the Right of Citizens of the Union and Their Family Members to Move and Reside Freely within the Territory of the Member States Amending Regulation (EEC) No. 1612/68 and Repealing Directives 64/221/EEC, 68/360/EEC, 72/194/EEC, 73/148/EEC, 75/34/EEC, 75/35/EEC, 90/364/EEC, 90/365/EEC and 93/96/EEC. O. J. L 158, 30.4.2004, pp. 77–113, 2 https://eur-lex.europa.eu/legal-content/PL/TXT/?uri=celex%3A32004L0038.

Directive (EU) 2013/32/EU of the European Parliament and of the Council of 26 June 2013 on Common Procedures for Granting and Withdrawing International Protection(Recast), O. J. L 180, 29/06/2013, pp. 60–95, https://eur-lex.europa.eu/legal-content/en/TXT/?uri=celex%3A32013L0032.

Directive (EU) 2013/33/EU of the European Parliament and of the Council of 26 June 2013 Laying down Standards for the Reception of Applicants for International Protection (Recast). O. J. L 180/96 29.6.2013, pp. 96–116, https://eur-lex.europa.eu/legal-content/EN/TXT/?uri=CELEX:32019L0882.

Directive 2014/50/EU of the European Parliament and of the Council of 16 April 2014 on Minimum Requirements for Enhancing Worker Mobility between Member States by Improving the Acquisition and Preservation of Supplementary Pension Rights. O. J. L 128, 30.4.2014, p. 1–7, https://eur-lex.europa.eu/eli/dir/2014/50/oj.

Regulation (EU) 2024/1356 of the European Parliament and of The Council of 14 May 2024 introducing the screening of third-country nationals at the external borders and amending Regulations (EC) No. 767/2008, (EU) 2017/2226, (EU) 2018/1240 and (EU) 2019/817. O. J. L, 2024/1356, 22.5.2024, https://eur-lex.europa.eu/legal-content/EN/TXT/?uri=CELEX%3A32024R1356

Regulation (EU) 2024/1351 of the European Parliament and of The Council of 14 May 2024 on asylum and migration management, amending Regulations (EU) 2021/1147 and (EU) 2021/1060 and repealing Regulation (EU) No. 604/2013. O. J. 2024/1351, 22.5.2024 https://eur-lex.europa.eu/eli/reg/2024/1351/oj.

Regulation (EU) 2024/1348 the European Parliament and of The Council of 14 May 2024 establishing a common procedure for international protection in the Union and repealing Directive 2013/32/EU. O. J. L, 2024/1348, 22.5.2024, ELI: http://data.europa.eu/eli/reg/2024/1348/oj.

Regulation (EU) 2024/1349 of the European Parliament and of the Council of 14 May 2024 establishing a return border procedure, and amending Regulation (EU) 2021/1148 1, 2024/1349, 22.5.2024, https://eur-lex.europa.eu/eli/reg/2024/1349/oj.

Regulation (EU) 2024/1349 of the European Parliament and of the Council of 14 May 2024 establishing a return border procedure, and amending Regulation (EU) 2021/1148. O. J. L, 2024/1349, 22.5.2024, https://eur-lex.europa.eu/eli/reg/2024/1349/oj.

Regulation (EU) 2024/1358 of the European Parliament and of the Council of 14 May 2024 on the establishment of "Eurodac" for the comparison of biometric data in order to effectively apply Regulations (EU) 2024/1351 and (EU) 2024/1350 of the European Parliament and of the Council and Council Directive 2001/55/EC and to identify illegally staying third-country nationals and stateless persons and on requests for the comparison with Eurodac data by Member States' law enforcement authorities and Europol for law enforcement purposes, amending Regulations (EU) 2018/1240 and (EU) 2019/818 of the European Parliament and of the Council and repealing Regulation (EU) No. 603/2013 of the European Parliament and of the Council. O. J. L, 2024/1358, 22.5.2024, ELI: http://data.europa.eu/eli/reg/2024/1358/oj

Directive (EU) 2024/1346 of the European Parliament and of the Council of 14 May 2024 laying down standards for the reception of applicants for international protection. O. J. L, 2024/1346, 22.5.2024, https://eur-lex.europa.eu/eli/dir/2024/1346/oj.

Regulation (EU) 2024/1347 of the European Parliament and of the Council of 14 May 2024 on standards for the qualification of third-country nationals or stateless persons as beneficiaries of international protection, for a uniform status for refugees or for persons eligible for subsidiary protection and for the content of the protection granted, amending Council Directive 2003/109/EC and repealing Directive 2011/95/EU of the European Parliament and of the Council. O. J. L, 2024/1347, 22.5.2024, ELI: http://data.europa.eu/eli/reg/2024/1347/oj

Regulation (EU) 2024/1350 of the European Parliament and of the Council of 14 May 2024 establishing a Union Resettlement and Humanitarian Admission Framework, and amending Regulation (EU) 2021/1147. O. J. L, 2024/1350, 22.5.2024, https://eur-lex.europa.eu/eli/reg/2024/1350.

Regulation (EU) 2024/1352 of the European Parliament and of the Council of 14 May 2024 amending Regulations (EU) 2019/816 and (EU) 2019/818 for the purpose of introducing the screening of third-country nationals at the external borders. O. J. L, 2024/1352, 22.5.2024, ELI: http://data.europa.eu/eli/reg/2024/1352/oj

Other EU documents

Council of the European Union. Council Conclusions on Mainstreaming Ageing in Public Policies, Outcome of Proceedings, General Secretariat of the Council to Delegations, Brussels, 12 March 2021 6976/21, SOC

142, 2021. https://data.consilium.europa.eu/doc/document/ST-6976-2021-INIT/en/pdf.

European Commission. Commission Staff Working Document. Applying the Human Rights Based Approach to International Partnerships An Updated Toolbox for Placing Rights-Holders at the Centre of EU's Neighbourhood, Development and International Cooperation, Brussels, 30.6.2021 SWD(2021) 179 Final, 2021. https://international-partnerships.ec.europa.eu/document/download/54c77670-4179-49f0-9af3-d1b18ff2d41f_en?filename=swd-2021-human-right-based.

European Commission. Communication from the Commission on a New Pact on Migration and Asylum Brussels, 23.9.2020 COM(2020) 609 Final. European Union, 2020. https://eur-lex.europa.eu/legal-content/EN/TXT/HTML/?uri=CELEX:52020DC0609.

European Commission. Green Paper on Ageing: Fostering Solidarity and Responsibility between Generations, 27 January 2021 COM(2021) 50 Final. European Union, 2021. https://ec.europa.eu/info/sites/default/files/1_en_act_part1_v8_0.pdf.

European Economic and Social Committee. *Coordination of Social Security Schemes between the European Union and Euromed Countries :Study*. LU: Publications Office, 2016. https://data.europa.eu/doi/10.2864/94071.

European Union Agency for Asylum. *EUAA Strategy on Vulnerability: A Harmonised Approach to Vulnerability in the Framework of the Common European Asylum System : November 2023*. LU: Publications Office, 2023. https://data.europa.eu/doi/10.2847/582590.

European Union Agency for Asylum. *Guidance on Vulnerability in Asylum and Reception: Operational Standards and Indicators*. LU: Publications Office, 2024. https://data.europa.eu/doi/10.2847/110546.

Other documents

UNDESA. United Nations Statistic Division. Recommendations on Statistics of International Migration, Revision 1, Series M, Statistical Papers No. 58. United Nations, 1998. https://unstats.un.org/unsd/publication/seriesm/seriesm_58rev1e.pdf.

UNDESA. Leaving No One Behind: The Imperative of Inclusive Development Report on the World Social Situation 2016. United Nations, 2016. https://www.un.org/esa/socdev/rwss/2016/full-report.pdf.

UNDG. The Human Rights Based Approach to Development Cooperation Towards a Common Understanding Among UN Agencies. 2003. https://unsdg.un.org/resources/human-rights-based-approach-development-cooperation-towards-common-understanding-among-un.

UNDP. What Does It Mean to Leave No One Behind? A UNDP discussion paper and framework for implementation, July 2018, https://www.undp.org/sites/g/files/zskgke326/files/publications/Discussion_Paper_LNOB_EN_lres.pdf.

UNDP. Discussion Paper and Framework for Implementation July 2018, 2018. https://www.undp.org/publications/what-does-it-mean-leave-no-one-behind.

UNECE. Guidelines for Mainstreaming Ageing. Geneva: United Nations Economic Commission for Europe, 2021. https://unece.org/sites/default/files/2021-03/ECE-WG.1-37_Guidelines_for-Mainstreaming_Ageing_1.pdf.

UNECE, Rome Ministerial Declaration A Sustainable World for All Ages: Joining Forces for Solidarity and Equal Opportunities Throughout Life MIPPA 20, 16–17 June 2022, https://unece.org/sites/default/files/2022-06/Rome__Ministerial_Declaration.pdf.

UNGA. Conceptual Framework of a Programme for the Preparation and Observance of the International Year of Older Persons in 1999 : Report of the Secretary-General, A/50/114 22 March 1995, https://digitallibrary.un.org/record/177179.

UNHCR. UNHCR's Policy on Older Refugees (UNHCR, 19 April 2000), EC/50/SC/CRP.1.

UNHCR. The 10-Point Plan in Action, 2016 – Glossary, December 2016, https://www.refworld.org/docid/59e99eb94.html.

UNHCR. UNHCR Policy on Age, Gender and Diversity, 2018. https://www.refworld.org/docid/5bb628ea4.html.

UNHCR. Emergency Handbook. Older Persons, 2020. https://emergency.unhcr.org/protection/persons-risk/older-persons#_ga=2.195038444.1980655889.1684257370-604704032.1684257370.

UNHCR. Working with Older Persons in Forced Displacement, 2021. https://www.refworld.org/cgi-bin/texis/vtx/rwmain?page=search&docid=4ee72aaf2&skip=0&query=need%20to%20know%20guidance%20older%20people&_gl=1*1i3b67o*_rup_ga*MTc4NjcwODA4My4xNzAzMjc3MTk5*_rup_ga_EVDQTJ4LMY*MTcwNjQ2MTg5MC4xNC4xLjE3MDY0NjIxNzYuMC4wLjA.

UN OHCHR and Global Migration Group. Principles and Practical Guidance on the Protection of the Human Rights of Migrants in Vulnerable Situations. Report of the United Nations High Commissioner for Human Rights, 3 January 2018, A/HRC/37/34. Geneva, 2018. https://ap.ohchr.org/documents/dpage_e.aspx?si=A%2FHRC%2F37%2F34.

UN Secretary General. Compilation of Guidelines on the Form and Content of Reports to Be Submitted by States Parties to the International Human Rights Treaties Report of the Secretary-General, 2009. https://digitallibrary.un.org/record/600446.

UN Secretary General. Analytical Study on the Promotion and Protection of the Rights of Older Persons in the Context of Climate Change Report of the Office of the United Nations High Commissioner for Human Rights, 30 April 2021, A/HRC/47/46, 2021.

UN Secretary General. Follow-up to the Second World Assembly on Ageing Report of the Secretary-General, 22 July 2011, A/66/173. United Nations General Assembly, 2011. https://www.un.org/development/desa/ageing/resources/general-assembly-reports.html.

UN Secretary General. Status of the Human Rights Treaty Body System. Report of the Secretary-General, A/74/643. United Nations General Assembly, January 2020, https://digitallibrary.un.org/record/3849276.

United Nations Network on Migration. Guidance on Bilateral Labour Migration Agreements. United Nations, 2022. https://www.ilo.org/global/topics/labour-migration/publications/WCMS_837529/lang--en/index.htm.

Reports

Age Platform Europe. The Right to Work in Old Age: How the EU Employment Framework Directive Still Leaves Older Workers behind, March 2021, https://www.age-platform.eu/barometer-2023/end-age-discrimination-in-employment/.

Age Platform Europe. Ukraine: The "Oldest" Humanitarian Crisis in the World, 15 March 2022, https://www.age-platform.eu/special-briefing/ukraine-%E2%80%98oldest%E2%80%99-humanitarian-crisis-world.

Age Platform Europe. Support for Older People in the Labour Market, 2023. https://www.age-platform.eu/barometer-2023/end-age-discrimination-in-employment/.

European Union Agency for Fundamental Rights. *Fundamental Rights of Migrants in an Irregular Situation in the European Union: Comparative Report.* LU: Publications Office, 2011. https://data.europa.eu/doi/10.2811/19312.

HelpAge International. Older Refugees at Heightened Risk of Exclusion as COVID-19 Continues to Strike the Americas. HelpAge International, 2021. https://www.helpage.org/news/older-refugees-at-heightened-risk-of-exclusion-as-covid19-continues-to-strike-the-americas/.

HelpAge International. The Impact of War on Older People (in Ukraine and Everywhere Else). https://www.helpage.org, 13 April 2022. https://www.helpage.org/newsroom/latest-news/the-impact-of-war-on-older-people-in-ukraine-and-everywhere-else/.

International Organization for Migration, *World Migration Report 2022*, Geneva 2021.

NGO Committee on Ageing- Geneva. The Rights of Older Persons in the Global Compact on Refugees Submitted by the NGO Committee on Ageing, Geneva, 2018. https://ageingcommitteegeneva.org/resources/documents/.

UNHCR. *Global Report. The Stories behind the Numbers.* Geneva, 2021. https://reporting.unhcr.org/global-report-2021.

UNHCR Age, *Gender and Diversity (AGD) and Intersectionality.* Geneva, 2023, https://www.unhcr.org/age-gender-diversity/.

UNHCR, and HelpAge International. A Claim to Dignity: Ageing on the Move. Regional Assessment on the Situation and Needs of Older Persons on the Move in the Americas. Geneva, 2021. https://www.unhcr.org/media/claim-dignity-ageing-move.

UNHCR and IDC. *Vulnerability Screening Tool – Identifying and addressing vulnerability: a tool for asylum and migration systems*, 2016. https://www.unhcr.org/media/unhcr-idc-vulnerability-screening-tool-identifying-and-addressing-vulnerability-tool-asylum.

World Population Prospects 2022: Summary of Results. New York: United Nations, 2022.

World Social Report: Leaving No One behind in an Ageing World. No. E.23.IV.2. New York, NY: United Nations, 2023.

WHO. Global Report on Ageism. Geneva, 18 March 2021. https://www.who.int/teams/social-determinants-of-health/demographic-change-and-healthy-ageing/combatting-ageism/global-report-on-ageism.

Other documents

Council of Europe. Digest of the Case Law of the European Committee of Social Rights, 2022.

Council of Europe, ECSR. Rules of the European Committee of Social Rights, Amended during the 328th Session on 6 July 2022, https://www.coe.int/en/web/european-social-charter/ingos-engagement-with-ecsr#{%2257676066%22:[4],%2258046116%22:[1]}.

Council of Europe/ European Court of Human Rights. Guide on Article 14 of the European Convention on Human Rights and on Article 1 of Protocol No. 12 to the Convention, Prohibition of Discrimination, 31 August 2022, https://www.echr.coe.int/documents/d/echr/Guide_Art_14_Art_1_Protocol_12_ENG.

Council of Europe/ European Court of Human Rights. Guide on the Case-Law of the European Convention on Human Rights. Immigration. 31 August 2022, https://ks.echr.coe.int/documents/d/echr-ks/guide_immigration_eng.s

European Commission against Racism and Intolerance (ECRI). General Policy Recommendation No. 16 on Safeguarding Irregularly Present Migrants from Discrimination. Council of Europe, 2016. https://www.coe.int/en/web/european-commission-against-racism-and-intolerance/recommendation-no.16.

European Network Against Racism. Racism and Discrimination in Europe in the Context of the Migration in Europe. ENAR Shadow Report 2015–2016. Brussels, 2017. https://www.enar-eu.org/wp-content/uploads/shadowreport_2015x2016_long_low_res.pdf.

FRA, ed. *Shifting Perceptions: Towards a Rights-Based Approach to Ageing*. Focus / FRA, European Union Agency for Fundamental Rights. Luxembourg: Publications Office of the European Union, 2018. https://doi.org/10.2811/533946.

International Labour Organisation (ILO), *Extending Social Protection to Migrant Workers, Refugees and Their Families: A Guide for Policymakers and Practitioners*. Genève2021.

Inter-Committee Technical Working Group. Harmonized Guidelines on Reporting under the International Human Rights Treaties, Including Guidelines on a Common Core Document and Treaty-Specific Documents, Report of the Inter-Committee Technical Working Group, 2006. https://digitallibrary.un.org/record/600446.

International Law Commission. Report of the International Law Commission Seventy-First Session (29 April–7 June and 8 July–9 August 2019), 2019.

International Organization for Migration. *Glossary on Migration*. Vol. 34. International Migration Law. Geneva, 2019.

International Organization for Migration's Global Migration Data Analysis Centre. Migration Data Portal, 2022. https://www.migrationdataportal.org/themes/older-persons-and-migration.

Internationales Arbeitsamt, ed. *ILO Multilateral Framework on Labour Migration: Non-Binding Principles and Guidelines for a Rights-Based Approach to Labour Migration*. Geneva: International Labour Office, 2006.

OECD/OCDE and European Commission/Commission européenne. Immigrant Civic Engagement and Social Integration, 2023.

OECD/European Commission. Integration of the Elderly Immigrant Population, in: Indicators of Immigrant Integration. Paris, 2023. https://www.oecd-ilibrary.org/docserver/044e2698-en.pdf?expires=1703869677&id=id&accname=guest&checksum=8B8068507F193D88770A79E3D70C79D6.

Statista. Mortality and Life Expectancy Statistics: Life Expectancy by Continent and Gender 2022. Statista Research Centre 20 October 2022, 2022. https://ec.europa.eu/eurostat/statistics-explained/index.php?title=Mortality_and_life_expectancy_statistics

UNESCO. Decisions Adopted by the Executive Board at Its 104th Session, Paris, 24 April–9 June 1978, https://unesdoc.unesco.org/ark:/48223/pf0000028409.locale=en.

Ius, Lex et Res Publica
Studies in Law, Philosophy and Political Cultures

Edited by
Barbara Janusz-Pohl
Anna Jaron

Vol. 1 Anna Jaron: Socio-Economic Constitutional Rights in Democratisation Processes. An Account of the Constitutional Dialogue Theory. 2012.

Vol. 2 Stanisław Filipowicz: Democracy – The Power of Illusion. 2013.

Vol. 3 Teresa Dukiet-Nagórska (ed.): The Postulates of Restorative Justice and the Continental Model of Criminal Law. As Illustrated by Polish Criminal Law 2014.

Vol. 4 Agnieszka Kupzok: Enforcement of Patents on Geographically Divisible Inventions. An Inquiry into the Standard of Substantive Patent Law Infringement in Cross-Border Constellations. 2015.

Vol. 5 Alicja Jagielska-Burduk / Wojciech Szafrański: Legal Issues in Cultural Heritage Management. A Polish Perspective. 2016.

Vol. 6 Maciej Mataczyński (ed.): The Takeover of Public Companies as a Mode of Exercising EU Treaty Freedoms. 2017.

Vol. 7 Maciej Barczewski (ed.): Value of Information. Intellectual Property, Privacy and Big Data. 2018.

Vol. 8 Pawel Smoleń, Marcin Burzec: Introduction to Polish Tax Law. 2018.

Vol. 9 Łukasz Pohl, Konrad Burdziak: Judicial Interpretation of the 1997 Criminal Code Provisions on Self-Defence. 2019.

Vol. 10 Adam Szot: Judicial Review of Administrative Discretion. The Influence of Court Decisions on Administrative Actions. 2019.

Vol. 11 Michał Peno / Konrad Burdziak (eds.): The Concept of Modern Law. Polish and Central European Tradition. 2019.

Vol. 12 Leszek Leszczyński / Bartosz Liżewski / Adam Szot (eds.): Potential of Precedent in the Statutory Legal Order. 2019.

Vol. 13 Łukasz Bolesta: In Search of a Model for the Legal Protection of a Whistleblower in the Workplace in Poland. A legal and comparative study. 2020.

Vol. 14 Paweł Chmielnicki / Adam Sulikowski (eds.): New Perspectives on Legislation. A Comparative Approach. 2020.

Vol. 15 Marcin Burzec / Beata Kucia-Guściora / Paweł Smoleń: Agricultural Activity in Poland: A Fiscal and Legal Study. 2020.

Vol. 16 Magdalena Półtorak / Ilona Topa (eds.): Women, Children and (Other) Vulnerable Groups. Standards of Protection and Challenges for International Law. 2021.

Vol. 17 Josef Albert Fox: Die polnische Verfassung vom 3. Mai 1791. Hintergründe der Entstehung und der Außerkraftsetzung. Stellung Polens im Zeitalter der Aufklärung. 2021.

Vol. 18 Barbara Janusz-Pohl (ed.): Juvenile Justice Systems: Poland-Brazil-Portugal. 2021.

Vol. 19 Leszek Leszczyński: General Reference Clauses in the Judicial Process. Context of Legislative Intentions Interpretative Discretion. 2021.

Vol. 20 Francisco J. Campos Zamora: Das Problem der Begründung richterlicher Entscheidungen. Eine Analyse auf der Grundlage der Theorie der juristischen Argumentation. 2021.

Vol. 21 Aneta Skorupa-Wulczyńska: Language Rights of the Citizen of the European Union. 2022.

Vol. 22 Mateusz Osiecki: International Legal Aspects of Aerial Terrorism. Methods of Law Enforcement in Aviation. 2022.

Vol. 23 Vladimír Sharp / Gabriela Blahoudková / Jakub Handrlica (eds.): Law, Pandemics and Ownership Restrictions. 2022.

Vol. 24 Piotr Kasprzyk / Anna Konert: Drones – Future of Aviation Law? Interference of Public Law in Private Law. 2023.

Vol. 25 Szymon Pawelec (ed.): Consensual Procedures in Criminal Law – Comparative Perspective. 2023.

Vol. 26 Dorota Pudzianowska: The Statelessness in Public Law. 2023.

Vol. 27 Bogusław Przywora / Aleksander Wróbel: Formalised Access to Pre-jurisdictional Free Legal Aid. Analysis based on Example of Ukraine, Poland, Great Britain and Sweden. 2023.

Vol. 28 Ewa Dawidziuk / Patricia Panero / Anna Tarwacka (eds.): Family, Law, and Society: from Roman Law to the Present Day. 2023.

Vol. 29 Marian Grzybowski / Bogusław Przywora / Aleksandra Syryt (eds.): Free Legal Aid, Theory, Legal Basis and Practice. European Standards. 2023.

Vol. 30 Karolina Gmerek: Trial as a Social Communication Occurrence. Interactions Between Professional and Non-professional Participants of a Trial. 2023.

Vol. 31 Paweł Wiliński (ed.): Effective Legal Remedies in Criminal Justice System. European Perspective. 2024.

Vol. 32 Olga Sitarz / Anna Jaworska-Wieloch / Jakub Hanc : On the (Non)existence of the Right to Religious Freedom of Persons Deprived of Liberty. A Reconstruction of the Normative Standard Based on Polish and German Regulations in Comparison With Empirical Studies. 2024.

Vol. 33 Marian Grzybowski / Bogusław Przywora / Aleksandra Syryt (eds.) : Free Legal Aid – A Comparative Approach. Volume 2. 2024.

Vol. 34 Dominik J. Gajewski (ed.) : Functioning of Administrative Judiciary in the Context of Economic Changes. 2024.

Vol. 35 Barbara Mikołajczyk : Older Migrants – Vulnerable and Excluded. Searching for Visibility in Universal and European Laws. 2024.

www.peterlang.com

www.ingramcontent.com/pod-product-compliance
Ingram Content Group UK Ltd.
Pitfield, Milton Keynes, MK11 3LW, UK
UKHW021816051026
15470UKWH00026B/1384

9 783631 924600